THE NEW REFORMATION

From a portrait by Bailly

SADI NICHOLAS LEONHARD CARNOT (1796–1832)
Discoverer of the Carnot Principle

THE NEW REFORMATION

FROM PHYSICAL TO SPIRITUAL REALITIES

BY

MICHAEL PUPIN

OF COLUMBIA UNIVERSITY

AUTHOR OF "FROM IMMIGRANT TO INVENTOR"

CHARLES SCRIBNER'S SONS

NEW YORK · LONDON

1928

DEDICATED TO MY FRIEND

C. H. M.

CONTENTS

ILLUSTRATIONS

THE NEW REFORMATION

PROLOGUE

THE realities described in the following seven narratives are the realities of human experience. They are not realities in the sense in which the word " reality " is often discussed by metaphysicists and speculative philosophers. Abstract philosophical discussions are foreign to the thoughts which guide these narratives.

The revelations of science during the last four hundred years succeeded each other like so many acts of a cosmic drama. Each act revealed a new physical reality which advanced man's understanding of nature's language, the language of the cosmic drama.

The first act announced the heliocentric planetary system of Copernicus and Kepler; the second revealed it as a celestial structure, each part of which moves in strict obedience to ideally simple laws, the laws discovered by Galileo and Newton. These discoveries disclosed a new physical reality, the reality of visible matter in motion.

The third act unfolded an invisible physical reality, the reality of electricity in motion guided by laws which are just as simple as those discovered by Galileo and Newton. The names of Oersted and of Faraday will be forever associated with this revelation, which revolutionized the physical conditions of human life.

Maxwell, inspired by Faraday, gave a new interpretation of Oersted's and Faraday's discoveries, and foretold a new physical reality, the reality of electrical radiation. Hertz demonstrated its existence, and Maxwell's prophecy, that all radiation is electrical radiation, promised to become a new physical reality.

Guided by the two physical realities, electricity in motion and electrical radiation, and inspired by Maxwell's prophecy, electrical research soon discovered the granular structure of electricity and located its granules, the electrons and protons, in the granules of matter, in its atoms and molecules. The electrical granules, the structural units of material granules, were recognized to be the centres of all radiation and the primordial toilers in chemical reactions. The universe as a dynamic electrical structure is the physical reality revealed in the fifth, the most dramatic, act of the cosmic drama.

Temperature as a measure of the kinetic energy of chaotic molecular motion became one of the fundamental physical concepts when Carnot, a hundred years ago, discovered the law of transformation of the caloric energy chaos into an orderly activity of caloric engines. The sixth act of the cosmic drama revealed that Carnot's principle is the guiding principle in all transformations of non-co-ordinated into co-ordinated physical activities.

The organic universe on our terrestrial globe was revealed, in what is called in these narratives the seventh act of the cosmic drama, as a physical structure endowed with powers of creative co-ordination. It constructs out of the microcosmic energy chaos, like heat, light, and chemical energy, orderly structures performing orderly functions.

The physical life of man is the highest product of this creative co-ordination; to transform the life of humanity into a cosmos, a life of simple law and beautiful order, is the highest mission of human life in its broadest aspect. Can it perform this mission by the revelation of physical realities only? No, it can not; it must search for other realities which are to-day outside of the domain of physical science. This leads the narratives to the recognition of spiritual realities which, like the physical realities, are rooted in human experience.

These realities are described in the following seven narratives. Each narrative tells the story of one of them, but not exclusively; it also reviews briefly the realities described in the preceding narratives. This made each narrative a self-contained unit and as such it had served the author's purpose of a popular lecture on physical science. Hence these seven narratives do not succeed each other like so many chapters of a book, but in several of them there are familiar echoes of the stories already told. This overlapping of consecutive narratives is, perhaps, the most effective way of impressing upon the laic's mind the close relationship between the several physical realities which science disclosed during the last four hundred years.

These narratives are addressed primarily to persons who have not an elaborate scientific training; hence they speak in terms of a simple and untechnical language. It is hoped that by strengthening our understanding of the physical realities the narratives will reform our mental attitude and make it better prepared for the recognition of the truth that physical and spiritual realities are the fruit of the same tree of knowledge, which was nurtured by the soil of human experience.

THE NEW REFORMATION

I

THE AWAKENING OF SCIENTIFIC INDIVIDUALISM

RECENT discussions concerning an alleged conflict between science and religion bring back to memory the history of an old conflict between two mental attitudes, the scientific mental attitude and that of old theology. This conflict is very old, as old as Christian theology. It was during its early history a part, only, of the general conflict between ecclesiastical autocracy and individualism. Ecclesiastical reformation was the first manifestation of this historic conflict, and its success paved the way for the assertion of the inherent individualism in all activities of the Christian civilization, and particularly in those of science. The growth of scientific individualism was so rapid and its achievements so beneficial to the evolution of our civilization, that the scientific mental attitude and the scientific method of inquiry began, over two hundred years ago, to influence the mental attitude in all activities of the more advanced Christian nations, including the mental attitude of the

[3]

Christian theologian. This influence inaugurated a new movement, which may be called the new reformation. Its first triumph was achieved when Galileo and Newton revealed to the mind of man a new universe never dreamed of during the previous epochs of human history, the universe of matter in motion guided by definite and simple laws of action of matter upon matter. This was the revelation of the first physical reality. The occasional clashes of recent years between the scientific and the theological mental attitudes are a puzzling revival of the old and regrettable antagonism between science and theology. Since the scientific mental attitude and the scientific method of inquiry are a powerful driving force in our modern civilization, a better understanding of their history and aim is certainly desirable. This narrative is offered with the hope that it may contribute a little to this understanding.

The Scientific Mental Attitude is beautifully described in William Cullen Bryant's well-known lines:

"To him who in the love of Nature holds
Communion with her visible forms, she speaks
A various language. . . ."

Following this suggestive idea of the poet we may describe science as the interpretation of nature's language. This description implies two things: first, the method employed in conducting the inquiry which leads to the interpretation; secondly, the knowledge of the physical truth which the interpretation reveals.

The *scientific method* is the universally adopted method of observation, experiment, and calculation. Its simplicity and definiteness are strikingly illustrated by the well-known legend, which tells us how Archimedes found a solution of the problem which Hero, the tyrant of Syracuse, had placed before him. The problem was to determine how much silver there was in a crown supposed to have been made of pure gold. One day, while floating in the swimming-pool of the public baths of Syracuse, Archimedes suddenly thought of a solution. The thought occurred to him that floating is nothing more than balancing the weight of the body against the weight of the displaced water. That is to say, the weight of a body when submerged in water will be less than its weight in air, and the difference will be equal to the weight of the displaced volume of water. If nature's language, which she addressed to Archimedes, is correctly interpreted by this thought, then Hero's problem is easily solved. The rest of the legend about Archimedes's shouts of joy, "Eureka, Eureka," we all have heard from our teachers, who told us that Archimedes rejoiced because he had made an invention which helped him solve Hero's problem. But history says that it was a discovery which thrilled him and not a mere invention, of which he had quite a large number. Yes, it was the discovery of a new concept, the concept of "fluid pressure." He abstracted from the language of nature this new concept and located its position in the logic of nature. By logic of nature is meant the physical operation, implied in the concept "fluid pressure," which makes floating equivalent to balancing the weight of the floating body against the weight of the displaced volume of water. The original *observation* which Archimedes made while floating in the swimming-pool of the baths of Syracuse, his *experiment* of weighing the crown when submerged, and his *calculation* for the purpose of finding out the proportions of gold and silver in the crown, are the three separate steps in the scientific method of inquiry which he employed. His discovery of the concept "fluid pressure," resulting from this inquiry, may be called the deciphered message, the interpretation of the language and logic of nature. According to this mode of speech scientific knowledge means an understanding of the physical concepts and of their relation to each other in the logic of nature.

Archimedes employed the same simple method of observation, experiment, and calculation in all his work, which gave us the essential parts of the science of Statics. It is obvious that the method of Archimedes postulates a definite mental attitude which appeals to the language of nature and to human experience as the only court of appeal; it pays no attention to authoritative opinion. This mental attitude recognizes that this court has the only evidence worth considering, and that it employs the inductive method in arriving at a verdict. This is the scientific mental attitude, and Archimedes was its earliest representative. He is the father of Physical Science. Its most characteristic feature is individualism, that is freedom from autocratic opinion, hence its history is a part of the general history of individualism.

The work of Archimedes was not taken up again for nearly two thousand years. This certainly is one of the most significant facts in the history of European civilization. It throws much light upon the evolution of that civilization.

The period of the rapid rise and gradual decline and fall of the Roman Empire during the five hundred years between the time of Archimedes and the last days of that Empire offered no encouragement to the cultivation of the scientific mental attitude and the scientific method of Archimedes. The deductive method of Greek philosophy which the Romans followed was probably responsible for it; the fascination of speculative philosophy like that of Democritus, Anaxagoras, and Lucretius may also be responsible.

The next period of nearly fifteen hundred years in European history witnessed the rise of a new ecclesiastical and a new political organization in the European social order, the Christian church and the Christian empire. This period not only offered no encouragement to the cultivation of the

[8]

ARCHIMEDES (287–212 B. C.)
Father of the Scientific Method of Inquiry

scientific method which Archimedes had inaugurated, but actually opposed it. The causes of this opposition will be reviewed here briefly, but only in so far as they throw light upon the main thesis of this narrative. The aim of this thesis is to show how the individualistic spirit of the Christian civilization not only eliminated this opposition to the cultivation of the scientific mental attitude and of the scientific method of philosophical inquiry, but assigned to it the leadership in creative thought.

MEDIÆVAL AUTOCRACY

Church and state may be described as two human instrumentalities the mission of which is to co-ordinate the three fundamental activities of the human soul: the intellectual, the æsthetic, and the spiritual activities. Without this co-ordination there would be a social chaos, and such a chaos threatened Europe during the Dark Ages. Authority backed by power was the only efficient co-ordinator of the barbarous masses of the Dark Ages. Mediæval autocracy of the church and of the state was the inevitable result. The autocracy of the Christian church during the Middle Ages demanded

[9]

a powerful organization which was destined to become highly complex. The faith which it guarded became complex also, and thus lost the simplicity of the original Christian faith. Christ said to Peter, his favorite disciple, "Thou art Peter, and upon this rock I will build my church," and on the brow of the Vatican hill, where Peter was crucified, there is to-day the most beautiful edifice of the Christian art, testifying to the fulfilment of this prophecy. It proclaims to the Christian world that Peter is the rock supporting the foundation of the Christian church. But Peter was a simple fisherman of Capernaum, and the gospel which he preached was the gospel of a simple faith. Scientific theories of the ancients were not a part of this gospel; the spiritual and not the physical world was the field of his mission. He knew nothing of the dialectics of Greek philosophy which blossomed out during the Middle Ages as scholasticism, the favorite philosophy of the mediæval church.

AUTOCRATIC CONTROL OF KNOWLEDGE

The Christianity which Peter brought to Rome was not the extremely complex Christianity of

[10]

Rome and of its ecclesiastical dependencies during the Middle Ages. This Christianity pretended and had many good reasons to pretend that it had the knowledge of all things worth knowing not only in theology but also in philosophy and in science. It refused to draw a line of distinction between knowledge in the spiritual and that in the physical world, and it would not tolerate any dissent from its dogmatic teachings. It was this intolerance which issued its interdictum against Roger Bacon's new knowledge relating to the physical world, and against his Oxford lectures about it, and later kept him in prison for fourteen years during the closing days of his remarkable life. The great offense of this prophetic Franciscan friar of the thirteenth century was his audacity to proclaim that experimental science was the queen of all sciences, and that those ignorant of its methods were guilty of lamentable ignorance.

The scientific spirit of Archimedes, after a slumber of fifteen hundred years, woke up again and manifested itself through the soul of Roger Bacon, but it clashed with the spirit of mediæval scholasticism. The practice of observation, experi-

[11]

ment, and calculation, which Roger Bacon advocated, was considered a practice of the black art and condemned by the leading disciples of the scholastic school. It was suspected to lead to results which, in their opinion, threatened to undermine the Christian faith as interpreted by ecclesiastical authority. Roger Bacon's science was considered a black art, because it told people how, among other things, to make mirrors and lenses, and it is often credited with the knowledge of the telescope. All this happened over three hundred years before the telescope was first constructed and disclosed to mankind a new world of heavenly bodies. The establishment and maintenance of its power and authority were much more precious to the mediæval church than the advancement of new physical truths. Physical truth had small value in the eyes of the doctrine which regarded human life as a preparation, only, for the supernatural life to come, and taught that in this preparation man must be guided by the language of the divine spirit and not by the language of nature. These two languages were supposed to be foreign to each other. This explains the radically different mental attitudes of the theologian and of the scientist of the thirteenth century.

Intellectual activities which deal with nature's language and logic should, and we certainly hope that they will, lead us ultimately to a better understanding of spiritual truths. Their primary object, however, is and always was the truth in the material world. To reach this truth we must, according to Archimedes and Roger Bacon, turn to nature as our highest court of appeal and not to mere notions of ancient authorities such as the mediæval ecclesiastics demanded. The notion, for instance, that bodies fall to the earth because they have a horror of the vacuum above, or because they seek their proper place, meant nothing to a mental attitude like that of Archimedes and Roger Bacon. To a scholastic mind it was perfectly acceptable, because Aristotle was the author of that notion, and scholasticism bowed to ancient authorities, and particularly to that of Aristotle.

CONFLICTING MENTAL ATTITUDES

The conflict between Bacon's science and ecclesiastical autocracy was a conflict between two mental attitudes and not between science and religion. This old conflict is not dead yet, but one of the contestants is no longer the autocratic church of Rome of the thirteenth century. Its place has been taken by an influential party of irreconcilables in the Protestant church of our modern democracy. This party, like the scholastic philosophers of the Middle Ages, is making vain efforts to decide physical truths by arguments supported by the weight of ancient authorities. One cannot help seeing in these efforts a desire to go back to the methods of the orthodox theology of the Middle Ages, although there are no good reasons which will justify the existence of so strange a desire.

The mediæval church had good reasons for claiming supreme authority in all matters pertaining to learning, no matter whether that learning referred to the intellectual, the æsthetic, or the spiritual activity of the human soul. It had rescued many precious remnants of ancient learning and culture from the ravages of barbaric invasions during the Dark Ages of Europe, and had provided new nurseries for it in the monastic and cathedral schools. These schools were the cradles of the ancient universities, like the Universities of Paris, Bologna, Pisa, Rome, Oxford, and Cambridge. They all had originally an ecclesiastical character and were essentially a part of the mediæval church. The church was their guardian and was responsible for their material support and for their teaching. It is not surprising that many of the great teachers in these mediæval seats of learning were primarily theologians and only secondarily philosophers. The main object of their philosophy was to harmonize Greek philosophy with Christian theology of those days; to reconcile Aristotle and Plato with the Holy Scriptures; to evolve a universe which is in harmony with the visions of the ancient prophets. Their ears were deaf to the language of nature; their minds were closed to nature's logic; their speech was never addressed to the earth, as Job demanded, and hence the earth never taught them. Is it surprising, then, that they never paid any attention to Archimedes, and that they frowned upon new and to them unintelligible methods of inquiry, advocated by an obscure Franciscan friar like Roger Bacon?

The conditions of European civilization after the

fall of the Roman Empire would not permit the Christian church to contract its sphere of activity so as to become a simple co-ordinating instrumentality of the simple Christian faith. It had to become a guardian of learning as well as of the faith, and as such it had to assume the guidance of the intellectual and æsthetic as well as of the spiritual activities of its followers. The church exercised its guardianship like a stern parent, permitting very scanty freedom to the individualistic tendencies of its children. One can imagine what such a guardianship meant to the growth of scientific individualism! Individualism like that of Roger Bacon was immeasurably more annoying to the mediæval church than exhibitions of so-called radicalism on the part of individual professors are to a university president of to-day, and to his board of trustees. Individualism could find no place in an organization like that of the mediæval church and state, whereas in science it has always received a place of honor. Individualism is the first idea suggested to one's mind whenever the names of Archimedes and Roger Bacon are mentioned. Individualism is the prime mover in the progress of science. The conflict between the mediæval ecclesiastical autocracy and scientific individualism was, therefore, inevitable and is perfectly intelligible. But in this conflict the ultimate defeat of the ecclesiastical autocracy was also inevitable and is perfectly intelligible.

THE RISE OF INDIVIDUALISM

History shows that the weakest elements in the design of the mediæval ecclesiastical structure were, in the first place, the excessive load of responsibility for the cost of its maintenance, including the maintenance of the many seats of learning which looked to the church for guidance and support; in the second place, the irrevocable commitment of the church to the idea that there must be one universal church, employing one universal vernacular, the Latin language. This enormous ecclesiastical administrative apparatus demanded an acquisition of wealth the management of which was and had to be in the hands of the learned servants of the church, who directed the co-ordinating activities of the ecclesiastical machinery. The source of ecclesiastical revenue and resulting wealth

[17]

was supplied by the common people, but obviously they could have nothing to say about its management. Besides, their ignorance of the Latin language made them feel that not only the worldly wealth of the church but also the spiritual wealth of the Holy Scriptures, recorded in an ancient vernacular, were monopolies of the learned ecclesiastics. All this gave to the church an appearance resembling feudal aristocracy, which the common people thoroughly disliked, as the numerous peasant risings during and after the Middle Ages clearly show. Ecclesiastical aristocracy was repugnant to the mind of these people, who saw in Christianity a brotherhood of man in which all are equal before God. That was the great force which attracted them. The history of the Bogomil struggles in Bosnia shows that in the early days of the mediæval autocracy the Slavs of the Balkans were among the first to rebel against the fundamental ideas of the mediæval ecclesiastical aristocracy. Simplification of the ecclesiastical structure and return to Christian democracy were their aspiration. The rebellion spread to northern Italy and southern

France, where the Albigenses and the Waldenses had caught the spirit of the Bogomils.

Finally, England became infected with a similar spirit of rebellion. Here Wycliffe was its leader. He gave the first philosophical statement of the causes of this discontent. Wycliffe's statement can be summed up briefly as follows: The church must give up its wealth and worldly power and become Christ-like. The second indictment of the universal church by Wycliffe was the interference of Rome in the ecclesiastical affairs of England, many of which were subject to the authority of the English sovereign only; and the third was a criticism of the church for hiding behind the screen of an ancient vernacular the spiritual wealth of the Holy Scriptures.

Wycliffe was an Oxford man; he must have known of Roger Bacon's sad experience, who was also an Oxford man and lectured at Oxford less than a century before Wycliffe started there his pioneer movement of ecclesiastical reformation. But Wycliffe never referred to the hostility of the ecclesiastics toward Bacon's science. This hostil-

ity was a minor incident; it was a natural result of
the ecclesiastical structure which was dominated
by scholasticism, and Wycliffe attacked what he
considered the weakest parts of this structure.
What Wycliffe had in mind may, broadly speaking, be described by paraphrasing Lincoln's words,
as follows: Church of the people, by the people,
for the people; that is, an ecclesiastical democracy.
Such a democracy, long before Europe was prepared for a political democracy, was of course unthinkable from the point of view of the mediæval
church. Wycliffe's dream of it, though hazy and
vague, warned the church that a new spirit was
rising, the spirit of individualism, which does not
bow to ancient authorities, and does not recognize
the truth which is supported by nothing more sub-
stantial than subtle scholastic arguments. Wycliffe
was preparing the field for the cultivation of scientific individualism without knowing it; the individualism which Wycliffe preached was destined to
advance the philosophy of the older Oxford individualist, Roger Bacon.

John Huss, a Bohemian individualist, a contemporary of Wycliffe, introduced Wycliffe's ideas into

Bohemia, where the people received them with open arms, and established the national church of Bohemia, which was to be a reduction to practice of what Wycliffe preached. This was the boldest challenge which the ecclesiastical autocracy had ever received up to that time, and was met with equal boldness by the Council of Constance.

OPEN REBELLION OF INDIVIDUALISM

The most important event in the first chapter of the history of the Renaissance is undoubtedly the drama in which Wycliffe and Huss were the principal heroes. During the second chapter of this history there came the expected gradual emancipation of philosophy, of science, of literature, of the fine arts, and even of the simple Christian religion from the trammels of scholasticism and orthodox theology. To the orthodox theologian the progress of this emancipation must have looked like a funeral procession carrying mediæval scholasticism to a grave which promised no resurrection. Without scholasticism the ecclesiastical autocracy was like a mediæval knight without his steel armor, and there were many bold foes eager to attack.

[21]

The blow was finally delivered when in 1517 Martin Luther nailed his ninety-five theses on the church door of Wittenberg. The proud and mighty church which for many centuries had struggled for supreme authority not only in ecclesiastical but also in secular affairs of the state could not consent to the humiliating limitation of its sphere of activity demanded by Wycliffe, Huss, and Martin Luther. On the other hand, without this limitation no emancipation could be expected from the trammels of orthodox theology and of the highly complex ecclesiastical organization which was the nursery of this theology. Not reformation but ecclesiastical reconstruction, which made emancipation from mediævalism possible, was the real aim of these three originators of the great movement called the Reformation.

The emancipation came and it certainly led to the boldest intellectual and social upheaval in the history of mankind. It succeeded because the historical evolution of the individualistic Christian civilization paved the way for it, a way which in the course of nearly three centuries led gradually from ecclesiastical universalism to nationalism in church and state; from ecclesiastical guardianship to unhampered individualism; from the artificial modes of thought developed by the scholastic school to the natural methods of inquiry preached and practised by Archimedes and Roger Bacon.

The discovery of America by Columbus, and the vision of a new universe, which appeared to Copernicus soon after this discovery, were a welcome stimulus to the awakened scientific individualism of those days. But these discoveries were isolated manifestations only of that Christian spirit of individualism which supplied the moving force to the European Renaissance in general and to the ecclesiastical Reformation in particular. That spirit was born and bred among the Christian nations and was always a vital part of their Christian faith. It received its rigorous gymnastic training and discipline in the schools of the mediæval Christian church, which was its stern and autocratic guardian. But as soon as it had felt its power it began to address its youthful accents through the mouths of Wycliffe, Huss, Luther, and other prophets of succeeding generations. Its voice awakened the slumbering genius of the Christian nations. It is not a mere accident that the same century which listened to Martin Luther, listened also to Shakespeare, Gilbert, and Francis Bacon; was thrilled by the matchless art of Hals, Holbein, Leonardo da Vinci, Raphael, and Michelangelo; wondered at the astronomical achievements of Copernicus, Tycho Brahe, and Kepler; watched in spellbound admiration the first flashes of the flame of Galileo's genius. No other century in human history can boast of having discovered so many stars of the first order of magnitude in its intellectual and artistic firmament. Each one of these stars was a brilliant manifestation of the new spirit of that individualism which seemed to go out of existence when the last traces of Greek civilization disappeared among the ruins of the Roman Empire. No other civilization had such a Renaissance, but no other civilization had the splendid nursery which the mediæval church, in spite of its many shortcomings, had offered to the Christian civilization of Europe.

This brief description of the gradual unfolding of the Christian civilization will, it is hoped, explain why the development of the scientific mental attitude of Archimedes became dormant and waited fifteen hundred years until Roger Bacon made the first serious attempt to revive it, and why Bacon's efforts apparently failed. It also shows why after this failure two hundred years were needed to prepare the adolescent individualism of the simple Christian faith to exercise its power in the evolution of European civilization, encouraging individualistic efforts in all activities of the human soul, one of which was the cultivation of the scientific mental attitude and the scientific method of inquiry.

RESURRECTION OF SCIENTIFIC INDIVIDUALISM

As a striking illustration of the awakened activity of scientific individualism during the Renaissance, the discovery of America and what followed in its wake will be briefly described. The ancient astronomers believed that the earth is a sphere, and Columbus inferred from that belief that by a western voyage he could reach India and perhaps other still undiscovered lands. His inference was supported by several observations of mariners of the Atlantic who had found driftwood not known in Europe. His attempt to reach India by a western voyage resulted in the discovery of America; it was a new experimental test of the inference regarding the figure of the earth which the ancients had drawn from their astronomical observations. Encouraged by this discovery and by the knowledge which he had found at the mediæval universities of Bologna and Padua, Copernicus gave to the terrestrial sphere a hypothetical rotary motion around a fixed axis directed toward the celestial pole. This hypothesis eliminated the sphere of fixed stars rotating around the earth, which was an essential element in Ptolemaic astronomy. It fitted admirably into an ancient suggestion of Pythagoras, the suggestion, namely, that the planets, including the earth, revolved around a central luminary, and Copernicus designated the sun as this central body. The heliocentric system of modern astronomy was thus invented, and the invention appealed strongly to the imagination of the scientific man of those days, because it suggested a new and beautiful view of the universe. But it had its opponents also.

The opposition of the theologians is illustrated

by what Martin Luther said about it. He called Copernicus a fool who dared to contradict the Bible, and an "upstart astrologer who set his own authority above that of the Sacred Scriptures." The great reformer lost his temper, probably because Copernicus assigned to earth and man and even to Martin Luther himself a much more modest place in the universe than some proud theologians of those days were willing to accept. Humility was not always a cardinal virtue of religious reformers, but it was such a virtue of men with a truly scientific mental attitude. In the presence of God's eternal truth they humbly bow down and cheerfully accept any place which that truth assigns to them.

The criticisms of the Copernican scheme coming from scientific men of those days were reasonable. It was admitted that the scheme satisfied, partly, the requirements of a truly scientific method, because it was based upon the observations of ancient astronomers and upon their experiments as well as upon the historical experiment which resulted in the discovery of America. But it did not quite satisfy astronomical calculations. It was obviously an imperfect scheme, and the problem of making it perfect was solved later by the scientific efforts of Kepler, Galileo, and Newton. These efforts offer a beautiful illustration of the scientific method of observation, experiment, and calculation, first adopted by Archimedes and then again fifteen hundred years later by the Franciscan friar, Roger Bacon. Lord Francis Bacon, the great author of "Novum Organum," was a contemporary of Kepler and Galileo, and he undoubtedly had in mind the achievements of these two men and of Columbus and Copernicus when he formulated his rules for inductive sciences and philosophy. What he preached was the actual practice which had been adopted by the scientific men of his day who had followed the example of Archimedes. He must have known also the "Opus Majus" of Roger Bacon, who anticipated him in many essential points relating to the inductive method in science.

THE FIRST TRIUMPH OF SCIENTIFIC INDIVIDUALISM

The history of science covering the period between the publication of Copernicus's great essay, "De Revolutionibus Orbium Cœlestium," in 1543, and the publication of Newton's immortal essay, "Philosophiæ Naturalis Principia Mathematica," in 1687, describes a scientific progress with a perfectly definite end in view, the end being the last link in the chain which guided scientific thought through a period of two thousand years, from Archimedes to Newton. The definiteness of purpose was Francis Bacon's requirement for every true progress of human knowledge. Tycho Brahe, the great Danish astronomer, had a definite purpose in mind when he recorded the data of his numerous astronomical observations. He knew that some day they would be called as witnesses to testify for or against the validity of the Copernican scheme. This call came from Kepler, and the testimony which he extracted from these data was most convincing, and it was certainly beautiful in its simplicity. It can be stated briefly as follows: The planets, including the earth, revolve around the sun in elliptical orbits, the sun being located at one of the foci, and not in circular orbits as Copernicus imagined; the radius connecting a planet to the sun sweeps over equal areas in equal times; the squares of the periods of revolution of the planets around the sun are in the same ratio to each other as the cubes of their mean distances from the sun. This testimony, known under the name of Kepler's laws, enabled the modified Copernican scheme to give a satisfactory answer to the scientific objectors of those days. Never did man in his "love of nature hold communion with her visible forms" in a more sincerely affectionate fashion than did Tycho Brahe and Kepler, and never did nature address to man a simpler or more intelligible language. But did nature disclose also all her logic which was hidden behind the words of this simple language? She did not, because she could not; there were several concepts in nature's logic which had not yet become a part of human understanding. These concepts were hidden behind the phenomena of accelerated motions, to which the planets in their orbital motion around the sun called the attention of the inquiring mind of man.

The detection of new concepts in nature's logic is the greatest mission of science. It is the result of its efforts to solve new problems in science. Kepler's laws were not laws in the strict sense of the word; they were a description of the planetary motions and contained a clearly formulated scientific problem. The problem was to find an answer to the question: Why do the planets move in accordance with Kepler's description? Kepler's undying fame is due to the formulation and not to the solution of a great scientific problem. The efforts to solve this problem covered a period of one hundred years, and exhibited as no other inquiry up to that time ever exhibited the great power of the scientific mental attitude and of the scientific method of research.

The final solution of the problem revealed not only the beauty of a new physical universe, but also the beauty of a new philosophy, the natural philosophy which was inaugurated by Archimedes. The influence of this revelation upon the mental attitude of mankind, and particularly upon the mental attitude of the theologian, was so striking that one is tempted to call it the inauguration of a new reformation, the reformation of orthodox theology.

II

THE PHYSICAL REALITY OF MATTER IN MOTION

GALILEO'S DYNAMICS AND THE THEOLOGIANS

Up to Kepler's time motion of material bodies was not a subject of scientific inquiry. The science of equilibrium, first developed by Archimedes and perfected during the first period of the Renaissance by Leonardo da Vinci in Italy, and by Stevinus in Holland, gave man a scientific knowledge of the conditions under which bodies will remain at rest. But it told him nothing about the motion which resulted when these conditions were not satisfied. This knowledge was reserved for the century which started with Galileo and ended with Newton. Without it the universe was a hopeless puzzle, and nature's language about the motion of her visible forms was a dead language.

Galileo, while a student of medicine at the University of Pisa, and when only seventeen years of age, made his first scientific discovery which was destined to revolutionize man's ideas about matter in motion. While attending mass in the Cathedral of Pisa he watched the swinging of a lamp with long suspension, and timing it by his pulse he found that every oscillation whether large or small was completed during the same interval of time. Subsequent experiments verified the original observation; this was Galileo's discovery of *isochronism* of pendulum oscillations. No experiment was ever performed with simpler means, and no experiment ever yielded a result which was so pregnant with new mental concepts. The discovery itself did not reveal a new physical law, but it presented to the inquiring mind a new physical problem, the solution of which demanded the knowledge of a new concept in the logic of nature. This was the concept which was hidden in the accelerated motion of the planets; it guided the inquiring mind to the solution of the historic problem formulated by Kepler.

It is interesting to observe here that Galileo's teacher in medicine was Andrea Cesalpino, the celebrated physician and botanist for whom the Italians claimed priority over his English contemporary, William Harvey, in the discovery of the circulation of blood. Did Galileo learn from his great teacher that heart-beats and resulting pulse, which he had employed for timing the swinging lamp in the Cathedral of Pisa, succeeded each other at equal time intervals? History does not answer this question, but it does say that soon after his discovery of isochronism the pupil of Cesalpino deserted medicine and turned his attention to mathematics and physics; he exchanged, as a writer puts it, Hippocrates and Galen for Euclid and Archimedes. Intuition must have told him that his discovery of isochronism concealed a great problem, the solution of which demanded his immediate attention, but that without the assistance of Euclid and Archimedes his efforts would be in vain. So rapid was his advance in physics that in less than five years he mastered the works of his new teachers, extended the principles of Archimedes, which gave him the title of "Archimedes of his time," and formulated his experimental scheme for unravelling the hidden meaning of isochronism. A few words about these experiments and their results will illustrate Galileo's individualism and his interpretation of the scientific method and mental attitude which he had learned from Archimedes.

A swinging lamp is a body falling toward the ground and then rising away from it along a prescribed path, and young Galileo saw a resemblance between this motion and the motion of a body gliding up and down an inclined plane. This was the type of motion which he proposed to study. His mode of experimental operation and analytical reasoning was never surpassed in its character of childlike simplicity. A few simple experimental measurements of distances covered in a measured time by weights falling from the leaning tower of Pisa, or gliding up and down an inclined plane, furnished soon the irrefutable evidence that these motions were uniformly accelerated. This confirmed the simplest assumption which Galileo had made intuitively. In this kind of motion the velocity changes at a uniform rate, the rate of increase during the downward descent being equal to the rate of decrease during the upward rise. This is *the law of motion of freely falling bodies* discovered experimentally by Galileo—a simple operation of nature and apparently insignificant. All fundamental operations of nature appear to us that way when we understand them. The aid which this understanding gives us in deciphering the messages of nature's language displays its great significance. Galileo's explanation of the motion of a projectile demonstrated the full significance of his law. This motion was a hopeless puzzle to the Aristotelian school. Galileo's law supplied the new knowledge which explained to him his earliest discovery, the isochronism of the swinging lamp in the Cathedral of Pisa. It also suggested to him the invention of the pendulum as a measure of time intervals in pulse-beats and in astronomical observations. Our modern clocks are the offspring of this invention. Practical application of a new physical truth gives it a vigor which appeals strongly to human fancy and understanding; Galileo was not only a great philosopher, an ingenious experimentalist, a fine classical scholar, an artist and writer of exquisite taste, but also a brilliant inventor.

Prior to Galileo's experiments the weight of a body was always associated with the pressure which the body exerts against its supports. Pressure, weight, and tension were the only concepts

GALILEO GALILEI (1564–1642)
Laid the foundation of the Science of Motion

associated in those days with our ideas of force. Galileo's experiments were the first to reveal that uniformly accelerated motion results from the moving force which bodies experience when their weight is not balanced by the counter-pressure of their supports. *Acceleration* became thus the new concept associated with our ideas of force; a new understanding of the logic of nature. Wherever there is an accelerated motion there is, according to Galileo, a moving force, and wherever there is a moving force there will be an accelerated motion when the body is free to move. This was the logic in the language of nature which was addressed to Galileo as he watched the swinging lamp in the Cathedral of Pisa.

To discover a new concept in the logic of nature is the highest achievement to which the scientist can aspire. Galileo's experimental philosophy yielded many results which, on account of a new concept which they contained, were foreign to Aristotelian philosophy, and particularly his proof that all bodies experience the same acceleration under the action of their weight. This was diametrically opposite to the teachings of the Aristotelian school, the school of the mighty theologians of Galileo's time. Galileo was bitterly opposed to this ancient school, just as bitterly as was his contemporary, Giordano Bruno. Bruno's sad experience with the Aristotelians and his tragic end were probably responsible for Galileo's bitterness. But the Aristotelians avoided an open clash with the brilliant youngster of twenty-seven, whose convincing experiments with falling weights threatened to revolutionize the views and the mental attitude of the philosophers of his time. They listened with patient anxiety to the enthusiastic public applause which greeted the triumphal procession of Galileo's new and startling philosophy, but they never hissed. A new mental attitude and a novel method of philosophical inquiry, crowned by splendid achievements, commanded their respect and, perhaps, their silent admiration. Galileo forced them into open antagonism. The resulting clash has often been used as an illustration of the ruthless persecution of science by the church. But it must be admitted that the illustration was often a caricature rather than a faithful picture of what had actually happened. A word or two upon this historic event seems desirable.

GALILEO'S ASTRONOMY AND THE THEOLOGIANS

A Dutch optician had succeeded in constructing a telescope, probably first prognosticated by Roger Bacon several centuries earlier. As soon as the rumor of the new instrument had reached Galileo he constructed one with his own hands, and with it he inaugurated a new era in astronomy. Discovery followed discovery in rapid succession. Galileo's discovery of the mountains of the moon, of the satellites of Jupiter, of the phases of the planet Venus, and of the sun-spots, brought the Copernican scheme into the foreground more conspicuously than ever, and it reminded Galileo of what Giordano Bruno, his contemporary, had said about it. Bruno's quarrel with the church about the Copernican hypothesis was taken up by Galileo after Bruno's death. The church had a high regard for Galileo and regretted the clash, which ended in the condemnation of the Copernican scheme, because it disagreed with ancient authorities. The church understood clearly the difference between Giordano Bruno, the hazy dreamer and speculative philosopher, and Galileo, the experimentalist of rare vision and definiteness of scientific aim. The scientific acumen of the learned ecclesiastics of Rome understood also that it was still beyond the power of Galileo's dynamical science to eliminate from the Copernicus-Kepler theory every trace of scientific hypothesis. The ecclesiastics had some technical right to insist that this theory had a hypothetical foundation only. A century later the church regretted that it had exercised this right when it condemned Galileo.

Lagrange, one of the greatest among Newton's followers, said this about Galileo's formulation of the laws of falling bodies:

The discoveries of the satellites of Jupiter, of the phases of Venus, of the sun-spots, etc., required telescopes and patience only; but it required an extraordinary genius to unravel laws of nature from phenomena which were always before our eyes but the understanding of which escaped philosophical inquiry.

The same enthusiasm which was expressed in Lagrange's eulogy, over a hundred years after Galileo's death, was already alive in all parts of Europe during his lifetime. Even Milton, who as an orthodox Puritan believed in a literal interpretation of the Holy Scriptures, held the Tuscan philosopher in highest esteem. During a visit to Italy he records that he had

found and visited the famous Galileo, grown old, a prisoner [in his own house] to the Inquisition for thinking in astronomy otherwise than the Franciscan and Dominican licensers thought.

In the first book of "Paradise Lost" the following lines were undoubtedly suggested by Milton's historic visit to the blind and aged Tuscan philosopher:

> ". . . like the moon, whose orb
> Through optic glass the Tuscan artist views
> At evening from the top of Fesole,
> Or in Valdarno, to descry new lands,
> Rivers or mountains in her spotty globe."

At that time Harvard College was founded and, according to Cotton Mather, its incorporators invited the exiled Slovak bishop, the learned Comenius, to become the president of the first American college. It would be interesting to know whether theological considerations prevented them from inviting exiled Galileo to become the first professor of astronomy at Harvard.

Barberini, the famous cardinal, was Galileo's friend and ardent admirer, and when seated on the pontifical throne he showed to the great philosopher every mark of distinguished consideration. But the irrepressible individualism of the fiery "Tuscan artist," stirred up by bitter controversies with the Aristotelians of the Sacred College, made a clash with the Inquisition inevitable. It was primarily a clash between persons and not between science and theology. The history of this clash indicates quite clearly that Galileo's new science, resulting from his historical experiments in Pisa, had produced a most favorable impression upon the mental attitude of the leading Roman theologians. It will be shown later that the subsequent growth of this science created a cordial relationship between science and Roman theology during the eighteenth century. The clash could have been avoided if Galileo had known that it was not his discoveries in the heavens, but his simple experiments on the earth, which ultimately led to the irrefutable evidence, that the Copernican scheme as amended by Kepler contained the only correct description of the planetary motions in our solar system. This evidence was furnished by Newton; the church of Rome not only accepted it, but also permitted one of its most learned men to devote his intellectual efforts to its advancement.

THE NEWTONIAN ERA

Galileo has been accused of paying scant attention to Kepler. But his accusers must have overlooked that Galileo never deciphered the whole message conveyed to him by the swinging lamp in the Cathedral of Pisa, nor by the orbital motion of the satellites of Jupiter which he had discovered. Hence he was not prepared to decipher completely the message which the motions of the planets around the sun conveyed to him through Tycho Brahe and Kepler and, as Milton expressed it, through the optic glass of the Tuscan artist. Several new concepts were needed which remained hidden behind the words of these messages. A brief description of the scientific method by which these concepts were detected is desirable. They are the foundation pillars of modern physical science, and every intelligent person should have a clear understanding of their simple meainng. Such an understanding is easily reached by studying the history of their evolution. The following brief statement of this history is offered even at the risk of appearing somewhat too technical. It is the history of the great scientific epoch of the Galileo-Newton century. The influence of this epoch upon the mental attitude of philosophers and theologians of that time was due not only to its great achievements, but also to the method of inquiry by which these achievements were accomplished.

BIRTH OF THE SCIENCE OF DYNAMICS

Galileo's experiments revealed that the acceleration of falling bodies is not proportional to their weight, as the Aristotelians believed, but that all falling bodies, light and heavy, experience the same acceleration. Hence, if the weight is the moving force then additional concepts were needed for determining the quantitative relation between acceleration—that is, the rate of change of velocity

—and the moving force. Why do all weights, large and small, produce the same acceleration? What, then, were these new concepts which escaped the scrutiny of Galileo's penetrating vision? Newton answered this question when, mindful of Galileo's experiments, he discovered the new meaning of the concepts: *mass*, as revealed by the motion of material bodies, and the *momentum* associated with it when that mass is moving. Under ordinary conditions the momentum of each particle of moving matter, or, as Newton called it, its quantity of motion, is equal to the product of its mass and velocity. *The time-rate of change of that momentum in any direction equals the moving force impressed in that direction upon the mass particle*, was Newton's answer to the question asked above. This answer is Newton's second law of motion. He also called it an axiom, a self-evident truth. To illustrate: in freely falling bodies the weight of the body is the moving force, and, according to Newton, it is equal to the rate of change of its momentum relative to the attracting earth. Newton considered the "rate of change of momentum," whereas Galileo had concentrated his attention upon the "rate of

change of velocity," or acceleration. This enabled
Newton to obtain a quantitative relation between
moving force and acceleration which Galileo had
missed. But it required a century to pick up what
a genius had overlooked. It is obvious that many
ingenious experiments, including those of Galileo,
and many direct appeals to nature were needed in
the formulation of Newton's fundamental law. It
should also be observed that in the experiments
which led Newton to the discovery of the new concepts, mass and momentum, and to the formulation
of his second law of motion, Galileo's pendulum
played an important part. That historical lamp in
the Cathedral of Pisa supplied the guiding light to
Newton as well as it did to Galileo a hundred years
earlier. Newton was building a new edifice and he
employed all the sound building material prepared
by his predecessors. The plan of the edifice, however, seems to have been in his mind from the very
beginning, and hence the remarkable definiteness
of his philosophical operations. Consider now
Newton's next step.

A genius who had discovered two new concepts,
"mass" and "momentum," and had formulated

their relation to the moving force, as expressed in the second law of motion, could not help detecting intuitively another new concept in the logic of nature, which Newton called "action." A material body in consequence of its momentum can act; that is, it can produce by impact a change of momentum in other material bodies. In other words, the momentum of a moving body endows the body with powers of a moving force. All human experience makes this obvious. But Newton was the first to employ a definite measure for this action and to make it a part of a general law. Newton's second law suggested that the action of a moving body upon another body with which it collides is equal to the rate of change of momentum of the acting body, and that the body thus moved will react with a force equal to the rate of change of its own momentum. This reacting force Newton called the "reaction." Collision of material bodies is the simplest illustration of the obvious truth that during the interaction of two material bodies it is immaterial which of the two is assumed to act or to react. Numerous experiments on impact performed by Newton's predecessors and by himself demonstrated clearly that in all collisions between elastic bodies the total momentum is preserved; that is, the momentum lost by one body is gained by the other. In other words, the action of one of the colliding bodies is equal to the reaction of the other. This led Newton to the formulation of the general law which says:

"Reaction is always equal and opposite to action; that is to say, the actions of two bodies upon each other are always equal and directly opposite."

This is Newton's third law of motion. It was also evident to Newton that Galileo's concept of acceleration and its relation to the moving force can be stated in the form of a law as follows:

"Every body perseveres in its state of rest or of uniform motion in a straight line except in so far as it is compelled to change that state by impressed forces."

This is called Newton's first law of motion. Nature's language concerning the motions of its visible terrestrial forms was deciphered into an intelligible message when man discovered the concepts *acceleration, mass, momentum, acting,* and *reacting forces*, and detected their relation to each other in the logic of nature. Newton's three laws of motion are the content of that deciphered message. This gave us the science of *Dynamics*, the oldest and the simplest of all physical sciences. Newton's three axioms of motion are its foundation pillars, and one often wonders why so simple a science was not formulated many centuries before Newton. The answer is simple. The mind of man was polarized by notions which had their origin in arbitrary assumptions of ancient authorities, like Aristotle, and this made the ear of man deaf to nature's language concerning the motions of material bodies. It was not until the motions of the planets around the sun, as described by Kepler, made this language so loud that Galileo turned a deaf ear to ancient authorities and began to listen to *nature*.

GRAVITATIONAL ACTION OF MATTER

Newton not only deciphered the messages of nature's language, but he also selected the most severe instrument ever employed by man for testing its accuracy. That instrument was the solar

[49]

system and all its motions due to the interaction between its members. But the following question had to be answered first: What are the interactions between the members of the solar system and do these interactions obey Newton's laws of motion? In preparing an answer to this question Newton's scientific intuition and power of induction displayed an individualism which is unique in the history of science.

Newton found no difficulty in showing that the motion of the planets, as described by Kepler's second and third laws, can be explained by his laws of motion. That much Galileo himself could, perhaps, have accomplished with the knowledge which he had created. But to make the orbits elliptical and locate the sun in one of the foci of the orbits, as demanded by Kepler's description, was a different and much more difficult matter. That was beyond Galileo's philosophy. Even Newton's three laws of motion could not accomplish it without the knowledge of a new and most remarkable property of matter, the existence of which Newton detected by a prophetic intuition. The legend, for which Voltaire is probably responsible, says that this

SIR ISAAC NEWTON (1642–1727)
Creator of Modern Dynamics

knowledge was suggested to young Newton in his native village by an apple falling from an apple tree under which he was resting, and, probably, revolving in his mind the meaning of the experimental philosophy of his great predecessors, Archimedes, Galileo, and others. He who understood the language and the logic of the swinging lamp in the Cathedral of Pisa and of the orbit of the moon around the earth as Newton understood them did not need the falling apple to suggest this additional knowledge.

Galileo's researches and those of his successors made it clear that the weight of bodies and the force acting upon them when in motion near the surface of the earth were due to an attraction between the earth and the bodies. This is the interaction between the earth and the material bodies, and Newton's philosophy made it plain that in this interaction the action of the earth upon a body is equal to the action of the body upon the earth. Hence, when a body is falling toward the earth the earth itself is falling toward the body. This bold conception never rose in Galileo's mind. It is a creation of Newton's genius.

But if the earth and the material bodies on its surface possess this power of acting upon each other, then why should not every material particle in the universe have the same power? Newton answered this question by the bold assumption that gravitational action is a permanent property of every particle of matter, and that this action follows his three laws of motion. This assumption was the boldest leap into the depths of the material universe ever made by mortal man. His formulation of the mathematical form of his well-known law of the inverse square was a comparatively easy matter, because he knew beforehand that it must satisfy all conditions which will lead to the solution of the great problem formulated by Kepler, and Newton's law of gravitational action actually solved this problem.

But the solution was much more comprehensive than Kepler's problem, because it told us not only under what simple conditions Kepler's laws give an accurate description of planetary motions, but also how under less simple conditions in the solar system the motions deviate perceptibly from Kepler's description, owing to the perturbing action of one planet upon the mutual action between other planets and the sun.

The power of Newton's laws of prophesying planetary perturbations and of calculating their amounts furnished the most decisive evidence in their favor; the power of prophecy is the best test of a new knowledge. The terrestrial tides, the spheroidal form of the terrestrial globe, and other previously puzzling phenomena appeared in the light of the new knowledge, formulated by Newton, as perfectly simple things. The beautiful edifice which Newton started out to build was, therefore, finished and the many assumptions which, with prophetic intuition, he had employed as temporary scaffolding were taken down. The edifice no longer needed their guiding support.

Laplace, one of the most ardent admirers of Newton's great achievements, and one of the earliest successful interpreters of their meaning and power, declared that they would banish all empiricism from Astronomy, transforming it into a mathematical science. His "Celestial Mechanics" is a glorification of the power of Newton's natural philosophy. He, as well as Kant, believed it capable of tracing the evolution of the solar system from a shapeless nebular mass into that beautifully ordered system of heavenly bodies which, obeying Newton's laws, move with a precision unattainable in mechanisms constructed by human hand. Voltaire, courting, as usual, royal favors, counted Newton's achievements among the greatest glories of the times of Louis XIV. Halley, the most distinguished astronomer of Newton's days, and a personal friend of the great philosopher, was quoted by Voltaire as having said this of Newton: "It will never be permitted any mortal to approach nearer to Deity." This was probably a much more accurate reading of a scientific mind than any that Voltaire ever attempted. In Halley's thoughts, however, as read by Voltaire, the times of the second half of the seventeenth and the beginning of the eighteenth centuries were the times of Newton, and not of Louis XIV, as Voltaire called them.

Halley's enthusiasm was stirred up not only by the results of Newton's gravitational theory, but also by the scientific method and mental attitude and by the boldness of scientific imagination of the philosopher. Halley was the editor of Newton's immortal essay, "Philosophiæ Naturalis Principia Mathematica"; he was the first to read its manuscript and absorb its meaning, which, in addition to personal contact with Newton, his "affectionate friend," made him certainly familiar with the inner workings of the author's soul. He, a distinguished astronomer, was the first to recognize the great value of Newton's views concerning gravitational action and the usefulness of the law of inverse square. But he certainly did not consider the mathematical form of this law the highest point in Newton's achievement, or he would never have consented to the insertion into the "Principia" of the following sentence: "The inverse law of gravity holds in all the celestial motions, as was discovered independently by my countrymen, Wren, Hooke, and Halley." Newton proposed the insertion of this sentence voluntarily, and Halley accepted it, for the purpose of composing a dispute with Hooke and Wren, who asserted that they had also thought of the law of the inverse square; but they had never proved it by experiment, or even by a philosophical argument. With Newton the law was not the result of a happy thought or accidental revelation, as many scientific discoveries have been. It was the result of observation, experiment, and calculation, performed by himself and by many other earlier philosophers who had followed in the footsteps of Archimedes, Tycho Brahe, Kepler, Galileo, Huyghens, and others. A vast amount of material had thus been collected, out of which Newton's philosophical acumen and unsurpassed scientific imagination had abstracted new mental concepts, and had revealed their relations to each other in the logic of nature. This is the revelation which conveyed to man the joyful message that nature in every part of the universe, as revealed by the motions of heavenly bodies, is intelligible, and that she employed the same simple language and logic when she spoke to Archimedes in the baths of Syracuse, to young Galileo in the Cathedral of Pisa, and to Tycho Brahe and Kepler, when, with a watchful gaze, they recorded and scrutinized the paths of the planetary wanderers in the distant depths of heaven; an ideally simple message describing an ideally simple material universe. The world wondered, and is still wondering, which of the two revelations is more beautiful—the simplicity of the universe revealed by that message, or the beauty of scientific intuition and analytical thought which guided Newton in his deciphering of the message. It is not surprising that many philosophers consider this message the first revelation of a physical reality which forms the background of the universe; some have gone even so far as to consider it the only physical reality, but Newton was never one of these. The modesty of a truly scientific mind made him confess that he had picked up one grain, only, from the sands of the endless shore of the universe. He made the earliest attempts to pick up another tiny grain from the molecular, chemical, and radiation activities of matter. Did he not feel that within the beautiful order, the cosmos, in the visible universe, all due to the gravitational action of matter, there might be another physical reality due to activities of matter which are not as simple as its gravitational activity? This is the question which modern science is answering.

CHANGE OF THEOLOGICAL VIEW DURING THE
GALILEO-NEWTON PERIOD

Newton was very much averse to controversies and avoided them scrupulously. In a letter addressed to the Secretary of the Royal Society he said: "I see I have made myself a slave of philosophy, but if I get free of Mr. Lucas's business, I will resolutely bid adieu to it eternally except what I do for my private satisfaction, or leave to come out after me, for I see a man must either resolve to put out nothing new, or become a slave to defend it."

How different from Galileo, who liked nothing better than a scrap with the Aristotelians! How different from many men of modern science who liked nothing better than a scrap with the orthodox theologians! But how about the Copernicus-Kepler scheme to which the theologians objected in Galileo's time? Newton gave a final demonstration of it, and yet he was not afraid that the theologians would accuse him of heresy! He must have known that no Martin Luther would venture to call him a fool who dared to contradict the Bible,

[58]

and an "upstart astrologer who set his own authority above that of the Sacred Scriptures," and that there was no Inquisition ready to call him to account for the doctrines in his "Principia," for which there was no foundation in all the ancient prophets. Newton knew that a great change had come over Europe's mental attitude in a short span of time after Galileo's death; Newton was born in the same year in which Galileo died. The intellect of Europe had learned to appreciate the scientific method and mental attitude of Archimedes, so beautifully illustrated by the inquiries of Galileo and of Newton. It had also learned that Galileo had laid the foundation of a beautiful edifice of science, and that where he had left off his successors had continued. When this edifice was started, the dome of Saint Peter's in Rome had just been finished; Michelangelo, its designer and builder, died in the same year in which Galileo was born. When one genius had finished one of the most beautiful æsthetic structures of Christian civilization, another genius was born who started the building of an intellectual structure which was destined to vie in beauty with the edifice on the Vatican Hill.

Newton designed and built the dome of the intellectual structure, the foundation of which had been laid by Galileo. Newton is the Michelangelo of Modern Dynamics. The world watched its growth for a hundred years and gained much knowledge from the artisans whose loyal and thoughtful toil supplied the nurture of this growth, just as the former generations had watched during the preceding century the growth of Saint Peter's on the Vatican Hill. In each case the beauty of the edifice as well as the skill, discipline, and loyal devotion of the architects and artisans commanded admiration. The noble structure which crowns the Vatican Hill is a monument glorifying the æsthetic activity of Christian individualism; the other edifice was recognized to be a monument glorifying the intellectual activity of the same Christian individualism. They are the earliest monuments to the power of individualism which keeps alive the vital spark of Christian civilization. One will always remind us of the individualism of Raphael and Michelangelo, and the other of the individualism of Galileo and Newton. Can any other civilization boast of such apostles of individualism, born and bred within the tiny time interval of two hundred years?

It soon became obvious that there was a bond of union between those two noble monuments of Christian civilization. He who is familiar with Newton's "Principia" and knows its historic background cannot behold that noble dome on the Vatican Hill which is the pride of Rome and contemplate its historic background without feeling that there is a mission which these two monuments have in common. It is their mission to stimulate the spiritual activity of the Christian soul.

Emerson's poetical tribute to Michelangelo:

> "The hand that rounded Peter's dome,
> And groined the aisles of Christian Rome,
> Wrought in a sad sincerity;
> Himself from God he could not free;
> He builded better than he knew:
> The conscious stone to beauty grew"——

applies equally well to Newton.

Study the lives of the men who contributed their share to the foundation and to the crowning dome of the "Principia"; study the method of their patient work and their humble mental attitude; contemplate then the beauty of the meaning of the finished structure, and you cannot escape the conclusion that it has a definite and a very great spiritual value; perhaps equal to or even greater than that of Saint Peter's in Rome. Science, the fine arts, and religion represent the three fundamental activities of the human soul, and the highest beauty of Christian life consists in a harmonious blending of these three fundamental activities, just as the beauties of human vision consist in a harmonious blending of its three fundamental colors. Sentiments of this kind must have been at work in those days to produce the revolutionary changes in the mental attitude of the world with regard to the new science which found its highest expression in Newton. These changes manifested themselves in many ways. When Newton died the church buried his earthly remains in Westminster Abbey, and in his epitaph we find the words: "He was the glory of mankind." This was the sentiment of the English people and of their churches without regard to sect or creed. Was there a dissenting voice on the part of any people or of any church in any part of the world? There is one answer to this question which deserves an honorable mention.

Roger Joseph Boscovich was one of the most learned among the Jesuits of the eighteenth century. He was a young man when Newton died. Although a Yugoslav by birth and race, a native of Ragusa, in Dalmatia, he received his higher education in Rome. After completing his novitiate he pursued his higher studies under Jesuit teachers at the Collegium Romanum. Mathematics and physics were his favorite studies, and so well did he succeed that he became a professor in the same institution. He, if anybody in those days, understood the mental attitude of the Jesuit school, and felt the spirit of its science and of its theology. It is one of the most characteristic signs of the mental attitude of the Roman theologians of those days that a man with this background of educational training and discipline was among the first European scientists to adopt enthusiastically Newton's natural philosophy and to make many efforts in the direction of its application. What a remarkable spectacle it was to see this Roman theologian watching the sun-spots for the purpose of determining the sun's equator and its period of rotation; figuring out the form of the terrestrial globe, taking into account the gravitational and the centrifugal forces at work during the plastic period of the earth's early physical history; making elaborate mathematical formulæ for the enrichment of the theory of the telescope! The theologians of Rome had evidently long forgotten that some of these were the very inquiries of Roger Bacon and of Galileo to which their theology objected in days gone by. Their theology had profited by long experience. The oldest and the most exacting theology of the Christian church had become reconciled to a science, the beginnings of which were believed for many centuries to be inimical to the Christian faith.

One cannot help regarding this change as a reformation of the mental attitude of the theology of Rome. The leader of this reformation was Newton, the greatest reformer in modern history. Newton, the don of Cambridge, accomplished what Wycliffe, the don of Oxford, had failed to accomplish. Wycliffe, Huss, and Luther reformed the church, but its theology remained practically the same. One cannot detect an essential difference between the mental attitude of the theology of Martin Luther, eager to condemn Copernicus, and that of the thirteenth century which condemned the natural philosophy of Roger Bacon. The first visible change in this mental attitude was that due to the influence of the Galileo-Newton science.

The mental attitude of man is often controlled by countless tiny notions; it is as immovable as the stump of an ancient oak which grips the soil with countless tiny roots. Nothing illustrates better the inertia of the mental attitude of man than the everlasting antagonism between the mental attitude of Christian theology and that of science. To have inaugurated the gradual elimination of this antagonism is one of the glories of the Galileo-Newton science.

III

THE PHYSICAL REALITY OF ELECTRICITY IN MOTION

FROM GILBERT TO GRAY

JUST as the scientific achievements of the period which started with Copernicus and ended with Newton revealed a new physical reality, the reality disclosed by *matter in motion,* so the scientific achievements of the succeeding period began to reveal a new physical reality, the reality disclosed by *electricity in motion.* The achievements of this period were the result of a philosophical inquiry which was guided by the same motive, the same mental attitude, and the same method of work as those of the preceding period. The spirit of Archimedes guided both. The disciples of this school of philosophical inquiry called themselves natural philosophers. This name was probably first suggested by the title of Newton's immortal essay: "Philosophiæ Naturalis Principia Mathematica";

it certainly differentiated the disciples of this school from those of the school of speculative philosophy.

It is an instructive historical fact that the first truly scientific effort to study the electrical and magnetic phenomena was made at about the time when Galileo made his earliest attempts to discover the fundamental concepts in the phenomena of matter in motion. William Gilbert, the greatest scientist of England of Shakespeare's time, the physician of Queen Elizabeth, made that effort, and he is regarded to-day as the father of the science of electricity and magnetism. He was a contemporary of Galileo and belongs to that brilliant galaxy of stars which adorned the intellectual firmament of the sixteenth century, the century of the Renaissance. Just as Galileo put a new life into the science which Archimedes had created and which remained dormant during a period of two thousand years, so Gilbert revived the electrical science, the fundamental phenomenon of which had been discovered by Thales of Miletus about 600 B. C., and which lay dormant until Gilbert aroused it from its sleep of over two thousand years. The causes of this dormancy were the same in each case. Their awakening during the Renaissance was due to the awakening, resurrection, and triumph of scientific individualism, that is, freedom of scientific inquiry.

Gilbert's chief contribution to the electrical science was the introduction into the study of the electrical and magnetic phenomena of the scientific method of inquiry, the method of observation, experiment, and calculation, the method of Archimedes. Neither he nor his successors during the seventeenth century enriched the electrical science by new and epoch-making discoveries. That was reserved for the eighteenth century, the century of Franklin and Volta. The scientific genius of the seventeenth century, the century of Galileo and Newton, devoted most of its splendid efforts to the new science of matter in motion. The interest which Gilbert aroused centred around the electrical charges at rest and the various methods of generating them by frictional electrical machines. The history of the electrical science of the eighteenth century began with Stephen Gray's discovery of the epoch-making physical fact that an electrical charge moves freely and, as far as Gray could tell, with enormous velocity along threads made of certain substances which are known to-day as conductors. This discovery is the beginning of a new epoch in the history of the science of electricity, the epoch of *electricity in motion.*

FROM FRANKLIN TO VOLTA

Gray's discovery did not attract the attention of the natural philosophers which it deserved. Newton's immortal "Principia" and the physical reality which it had revealed dominated the scientific minds of those days; a generous appreciation of the full importance of a new electrical discovery made by an obscure experimentalist could not be expected from the natural philosophers who were spellbound by Newton's achievements. Newton himself was interested in electrical phenomena, and he had constructed a new type of frictional electrical machine; the importance of Gray's discovery would not have escaped him, but this discovery was made two years after Newton's death, two hundred years ago. It was reserved for Franklin

[69]

to direct the natural philosopher's attention to electricity in motion discovered by Gray.

The efforts of the electrical experimentalists of Franklin's time to produce as large an electrical charge as was possible with the electrical machines of those days led to the invention of the Leyden jar in 1746. Franklin modified its construction, substituting glass plates for glass jars, each side of the glass plates being suitably covered with metal foil properly insulated. This is the prototype of the modern electrical condenser. As its name implies, its function was to store up, to condense, a large charge by the action of the electrical machine upon the metal plates which are separated by a thin insulating glass plate. Franklin recognized that the proximity of the conducting plates, as well as the action of the insulator between them, increased the charge, which he increased further by connecting a large number of these so-called Franklin plates into a battery. Connecting the conducting plates of one side of the battery to the conducting plates on the other side by means of a conducting wire set the charge in motion, and produced the largest transient electrical currents ever produced up to that time. This was the beginning of Franklin's historical experiments with moving electricity, which in his resourceful hands produced most startling effects. They attracted world-wide attention when Franklin proved beyond all reasonable doubt that lightning is an electrical discharge between the plates of a condenser in which an electrically charged cloud formed one conducting plate and the earth or another cloud represented the other plate. Motion of electricity along a conducting wire, discovered by Gray, appeared in a new light, when the natural philosophers saw that such a motion can carry the destructive power of Jove's irresistible bolts. Motion of electricity took hold then of the scientific mind, just as firmly as motion of matter did when Galileo's experiments and their logic had carried conviction even to the reluctant minds of many orthodox theologians. Motion of large quantities of electricity became then the goal of the electrical investigators. Their thrill was, therefore, perfectly natural when they heard that Volta had discovered a new electrical generator which can produce motions of electrical charges much greater and much more easily managed than

ever before. The Volta pile, an electrical generator
of ideal simplicity, was the crowning glory of the
eighteenth-century electrical science which made
the names of Gray, Franklin, and Volta immortal.

FROM VOLTA TO OERSTED AND AMPÈRE

The discovery of the Volta pile is a striking illustration of the scientific method of inquiry. First
came the casual observation made by the distinguished Italian physiologist Galvani, the observation, namely, that freshly prepared frog's legs sus-
pended by a copper wire on an iron rod contracted
convulsively whenever they touched the iron rod.
He had previously observed the same contraction
when an electrical charge was applied to the legs.
This contraction was a message from nature's language, and Volta was the first to decipher it. He
inferred that an electromotive force was produced
by the juncture of the two metals through the fluid
in the frog's legs, and this force produced a motion
of electricity, an electrical current, when the legs
and the two metals formed a circuit.

This interpretation of Galvani's observation
suggested to Volta his historical experiments, which

resulted in the birth of the Voltaic cell, consisting of two plates of different metals immersed in a suitable fluid, usually a salt or acid solution. Observation and experiment led to a concrete result, a complete deciphering by Volta of the message which nature had addressed to Galvani. This was a new triumph of the scientific method of inquiry inaugurated by Archimedes.

The novelty and simplicity of the cell and its sustained propulsion of moving electricity were not the only virtues which attracted attention to this new electrical generator; its power to exhibit new electrical phenomena accompanying the motion of electricity won the great admiration of the natural philosophers. Chemical decomposition of the fluids through which it maintained the electrical current, the so-called electrolysis, was soon discovered. When Sir Humphry Davy, employing this new instrumentality, isolated two new elements, sodium and potassium, from soda and potash, respectively, the chemists recognized in the science of moving electricity a most welcome addition to the science of chemistry. This recognition of the chemists was exhibited in a striking manner when Berzelius and Sir Humphry Davy, the two leading chemists of Volta's days, advanced the theory that the electrical forces residing in the molecules of matter are the most powerful forces involved in chemical reactions. This assigned to the young *electrical science* a place of honor in the chemical laboratory. But it soon outgrew this temporary home, and moved into a home of its own, which grew bigger and bigger so rapidly that to-day it is offering a welcome roof to every one of the physical sciences, even to the science of astronomy, the science which interprets the language of the stars. The language of the electrical forces is to-day a new language of the heavenly stars. The language of the gravitational forces is not the only language of the physical universe, as in the Galileo-Newton century.

It was a chemist who moved the electrical science from the chemical laboratory to an abode of its own where it ruled supreme as a master science. This chemist was Michael Faraday, the son of a blacksmith, and in his boyhood days a humble bookbinder apprentice. While learning to master the art of his trade he attended at the Royal Institution in London the evening lectures on chemistry delivered by famous Sir Humphry Davy. There he received the heavenly thrill which aroused his native genius for scientific inquiry. The first to discover this genius was Davy himself, who employed Faraday as a laboratory assistant. Davy, one of the foremost scientific discoverers of his time, considered his discovery of Faraday the greatest discovery that he had ever made.

Davy's brilliant electrical experiments, employing very powerful Voltaic batteries, fired the scientific imagination of the world and certainly that of Faraday and of Oersted, the Danish physicist. While experimenting with large electrical currents, produced by Voltaic batteries of the type and power which Davy employed, Oersted discovered that electricity in motion produces a magnetic force in every part of space. This great discovery, the mother of electromagnetism, is the beginning of the epoch of the electrical science of the nineteenth century, which will be recorded in history as the electrical century. Faraday made it the century of great electrical achievements.

Oersted's discovery was the greatest scientific

sensation of the first quarter of the nineteenth century. It presented to the scientific mind of the world a new question, namely, what is the law which governs the magnetic force discovered by Oersted? An answer came, and the swiftness of its arrival thrilled the scientific world almost as much as the discovery itself. The French Academy was the first to hear the answer. This was not surprising; never in its history was the scientific glory of this famous institution as great as in those days. The scientific genius of France was never as brilliant as during the stirring period of the French revolution and of Napoleon's Empire. Laplace, Lagrange, Legendre, and Lavoisier; Fresnel, Fourier, and Poisson; Ampère and Arago were a group of scientific giants never equalled by any group assembled in any learned academy. They were the greatest glory of France in those stirring days. It was Ampère, a distinguished member of this group of immortals, who first deciphered the message of nature's language addressed to Oersted, and he deciphered it within a week after he had heard the message. A few simple experiments and a brilliant mathematical analysis revealed to Ampère the meaning of the message. He translated it into a simple law expressing the intensity of the magnetic force at any point in space in terms of the electrical currents which produce it. This extraordinary achievement astonished even Maxwell, the greatest mathematical physicist of the nineteenth century. Ampère's law will be stated presently in its more modern form.

FROM FARADAY TO MAXWELL

Oersted's discovery and Ampère's formulation of its fundamental law encouraged the belief that there is an inseparable bond between electric and magnetic forces. It was this belief which supplied the motive power for further advancement of the electrical science. The origin of this belief was probably in the intuition that just as the motion of electricity produces, according to Oersted's discovery, magnetic forces, so the motion of magnetism will, perhaps, produce electrical forces. Such a reciprocal relationship would certainly be a creation of extraordinary beauty, and a beautiful conception born by pure intuition often leads to a new revelation in the temple of eternal truth. He who found that beautiful relationship in this temple was Faraday, when he discovered that a varying electrical current in a conductor produces electrical currents in other conductors. Faraday immediately drew the obvious inference that a magnet moving in the vicinity of an electrical circuit will produce an electrical current in it and that, therefore, just as moving electricity produces magnetic forces, so moving magnetism produces electrical forces in conducting wires. He verified the inference by many experiments with moving magnets. This was Faraday's discovery of electromagnetic induction, which with Oersted's discovery of electromagnetism forms the foundation of the Electrical Science.

Plausible arguments have been advanced that Oersted's discovery of electromagnetism made Faraday's discovery of electromagnetic induction inevitable; that it was bound to come sooner or later. This, perhaps, is true. It was, however, very fortunate that Faraday was the first to make the inevitable discovery. No other man would have given it that wonderful interpretation which he gave it; his interpretation of the new physical phenomenon, electromagnetic induction, is in my opinion even more important than the discovered physical fact. When the achievements of Oersted's and Faraday's epoch-making discoveries are considered, one usually thinks of the visible services which they have rendered to the world, like the services of the dynamo and the motor, of the telegraph and the telephone, of electric lighting and electrical power transmission, and of many other electrical inventions which revolutionized the material well-being of man. These services reveal a new physical reality, the reality of electricity moving in obedience to ideally simple laws. We appreciate it, because we see it in operation in every nook and corner of our daily life, aiding us in our efforts to make each individual life and that of humanity a life of greater material comfort. It is a physical reality which may be called a terrestrial one, because it concerns principally our human affairs on the earth. Great as these visible material services certainly are, they are small in comparison with the invisible services of the new reality; one does not see them in every nook and corner of our daily life. The greatest among these invisible services is the message which announced that there is in store for us a revelation of a new physical reality in the universe, the reality, namely, revealed by the electrical activity of the heavenly stars. To this invisible service Faraday contributed a lion's share by his prophetic interpretation of the hidden meaning of electromagnetism and of electromagnetic induction. Faraday the seer was just as great as Faraday the discoverer.

Faraday's prophetic visions were not understood until his great disciple, James Clerk Maxwell, had revealed his master's meaning. Even then years elapsed before the world understood Maxwell's message. Can that message be stated to-day in simple terms which an intelligent laic with no elaborate scientific training can understand? Perhaps it can, and I venture to try it, fully conscious of the great difficulty of my undertaking. The effort is worth while, because Maxwell's message from Faraday revealed a new physical reality which in many respects was even more startling than the physical reality revealed by Newton's message. Every educated person should understand these two physical realities; they are to-day the two most essential parts of our knowledge of the eternal truth which guides the destiny of our physical universe and interprets its meaning. I hope that this statement, made in all sincerity, will persuade my readers to follow me in the short up-hill climb which follows.

FARADAY'S NEW CONCEPTS IN THE ELECTRICAL SCIENCE

The eighteenth-century concept of electrical and magnetic forces was that derived from the action of electrical and magnetic charges at rest. Coulomb's experiments belong to that century, and they formulated the law of action of these charges upon each other. The mathematical form of this law is the same as that of Newton's law of gravitational action of matter upon matter. In place of the material masses which appear in Newton's mathematical statement of the gravitational law of the inverse square, we have in Coulomb's statement electrical and magnetic charges. Just as the gravitational force meant a mechanical force of attraction between material bodies, so the electrical force and the magnetic force meant to Coulomb a mechanical force of attraction or repulsion between electrical charges and between magnetic charges, respectively. But Oersted's and Faraday's discoveries of electromagnetism and of electromagnetic induction, respectively, revealed magnetic and electrical forces the origin of which could not be traced to magnetic and electrical charges. To illustrate: Consider the magnetic force generated by the following simple arrangement. A Voltaic cell, consisting of a copper plate and a zinc plate immersed in a sulphate of copper solution, sustains an electrical current through a conducting wire connecting the zinc plate to the copper plate. According to Oersted's discovery, a magnetic force will be generated in every point of space, although there is no magnetic charge anywhere. Oersted pointed out that this magnetic force is vortical; it drives a magnetic pole around closed curves which are interlinked with the conducting wire. According to Coulomb's law, such a magnetic force cannot result from any magnetic charges. Consider next the electrical current generated by the following simple arrangement: A circular turn of conducting wire and a cylindrical magnet face each other, their axes coinciding. Everything is symmetrical with respect to the common axis. Move now the cylindrical magnet along the common axis; according to Faraday's discovery, a current is generated in the conducting turn. The symmetry of the arrangement makes it obvious that there is an electrical force in every element of the circular turn, and that it is uniformly distributed around the length of the turn. The symmetry makes it also obvious that there are no electrical charges on the conducting wire nor anywhere else to account for the electrical forces which propel the moving electricity. When an unsymmetrical arrangement is employed, then electrical charges will accumulate at various points of the conducting wire. But Coulomb's law says that no distribution of electrical charges on a conducting circuit can produce electrical forces, such as Faraday discovered, which will make electricity move around the circuit. Oersted's and Faraday's forces have a vortical character, and Coulomb says nothing about such forces, except that they cannot be due to charges. In the case of vortical forces it is more convenient to speak of their sum around a closed curve, a circuit. It is in this sense that Oersted's *magnetomotive force* and Faraday's *electromotive force* must be understood. They are the sum of the magnetic and of the electrical forces, respectively, around a circuit. The discovery of these vortical forces demanded new concepts which would include all electrical and magnetic forces, no matter what their origin may be, or by what effects they manifest themselves. These concepts, created by Faraday, the concepts of the electrical and of the magnetic flux, are the foundation of the modern electromagnetic science; I shall try to develop them, following as far as practicable Faraday's method.

FARADAY'S FIRST STEP

It is well to mention here that in the development of these concepts Faraday makes several distinct steps; I propose to use them as landmarks on the path along which Faraday will lead us. His first step, the first landmark, was the introduction of the graphical in place of mathematical method of studying electrical and magnetic forces. To illustrate: Consider the forces of any distribution of electrical charges. According to Coulomb's law the

From a photograph by John Watkins, London

MICHAEL FARADAY (1791–1867)
Father of Modern Electrical Science

charges will act with a definite force upon a unit
charge at every point in space. This law enables us
to calculate it. Faraday devised the following
graphical method to replace Coulomb's mathematical method. Imagine curves drawn in space in
such a way that the electrical force at any one of
its points will be tangent to the curve. These
curves, the curves of force, will enclose spaces
which are tubular, because no two curves can inter-
sect. If they did, then at the point of intersection
the electrical force would have two different directions, which is contrary to all experience and to
Coulomb's law. Imagine one of these tubes so adjusted that at one of its points the area of its
smallest cross-section has a ratio to a unit area
which is numerically equal to the electrical force
at that point. Call this ratio the "density of the
tube" at that point. It can be shown that at any
other point of this tube its density will again give
the numerical value of the force at that point. In
other words, where the tube is narrow the force
is large, and where the tube is wide the force is
small. All the tubes which fill the infinite space
can be adjusted in the same way, at least in our

imagination. At every point in space the direction and the density of the tubes will give the direction and the numerical value of the electrical force.

Observe now that the total number of these tubes is proportional to the total charge. This becomes obvious when we consider that making the charge in each one of its volume elements n times larger will make the force, that is the density of the tubes, n times larger at every point in space, and, therefore, the total number of tubes will be n times larger. This is Faraday's graphical representation of what is called the field of force of electrical charges, his first step in the development of new concepts regarding electrical and magnetic forces.

This description of Faraday's first step sounds very much like a discourse on geometry; nothing but curves. But very many of my readers are keenly interested in the curves described by flying baseballs and golf-balls, and they know that these curves suggest concrete physical facts: twirling, slicing, etc. I assure them that in the background of Faraday's curving tubes there will be found most interesting physical facts, which are the building-stones of our modern electrical science.

It appeared at first that Faraday's graphical representation of the field of force of electrical charges is only another way of saying the same thing which the mathematical formula of Coulomb says. This is true, but Faraday made his geometrical picture of the field of force say many things which Coulomb's formula never said. This brings me to the second step, the second landmark, in the progressive development of Faraday's concepts.

FARADAY'S SECOND STEP

Suppose that the charges are located on a material body which is surrounded by a vacuum; the field of force in the space outside of the charges will be in a vacuum. According to Faraday this space is a vacuum in the sense only that it contains no material bodies, but it is not a vacuum in the sense of containing nothing. It contains the tubes of force, and to Faraday these tubes meant more than a mere geometrical picture. According to him the tubes are a graphical representation of an entity, an ultra-material substance, the state of which at any point manifests itself as an electrical force at that point. That state is specified, as far as our present knowledge can specify it, by the direction and the density of the tubes. This hypothetical entity, called here the *electrical flux*, is the concept to which Faraday devoted more attention than to the particular process which produced the electrical charges and their electrical forces.

Faraday represented the field of force of magnetic charges in the same way and obtained a graphical representation of the *magnetic flux*. The magnetic flux, just like the electrical flux, meant to Faraday an entity, the state of which manifests itself as a magnetic force. The introduction of these two hypothetical entities, the electrical and the magnetic flux, into the electrical and magnetic phenomena was the first hypothesis which Faraday, prompted by his prophetic vision, boldly suggested; this was the second step in the development of his new concepts. Faraday never encouraged the view that the fluxes were necessarily manifestations of the luminiferous ether, the only ultra-material substance ever considered at that time. On the contrary, he suggested, on several occasions, that the flux of force might perhaps replace the luminiferous ether, which was so popular in those days.

It is, therefore, not surprising that the philosophers of those days did not follow him; they admired his great experimental discoveries, but his novel views puzzled them and they asked: If Faraday's fluxes are neither material nor ethereal, what are they?

FARADAY'S THIRD STEP

Faraday, the seer, had caught a glimpse of an ultra-material substance which mystified ordinary mortals. But he was not a mystic, nor did he intentionally mystify anybody; on the contrary, he illuminated his unfolding visions by many simple experiments. To illustrate: The physical fact that the charge in a Franklin plate produced by the action of a given machine is increased by employing glass or some other solid insulator in place of air between the conducting plates was observed and often mentioned by Franklin. Faraday's interpretation was that the increase of the charge meant an increase of the density of the electrical flux in the insulator. His historical experiments with electrical condensers consisting of two concentric spherical shells as conducting plates, insulated from each other, illuminated this relationship. When

[89]

the insulating material was air, the charge produced by a Voltaic battery was smaller than when it was glass or some other solid or fluid insulator. Faraday's experiments showed that for a given Voltaic battery the electrical force at any given point between the two concentric shells must be independent of the insulating material, but the increase of the charge with solid insulators meant that the flux is not independent. Faraday interpreted this experimental fact by assuming, in effect, that in solid and fluid insulators, like paraffin, glass, and insulating oils, the flux offers less reaction to the increase of its density than it does in free space, that is, in air or in vacuum, and that, similarly, magnetic flux offers less reaction in iron, steel, nickel, and in other magnetizable bodies than it does in unmagnetizable bodies or in a vacuum. In other words, these bodies are more permeable to flux than free space is. A reacting flux in a vacuum, as well as in material bodies, was the result of Faraday's third step. His hypothetical substances, the fluxes, as reacting entities were thus brought within the reach of experimental measurement, because an electrical or magnetic reaction is an electrical, or, respectively, a magnetic force, and such forces can be detected and measured.

Every concept in physical science must be capable of quantitative measurement if it is to be a part of a physical theory. When Faraday detected in the fluxes a power to react he made the first provision for their place in the physical theory which he was constructing on the foundation of his experimental discoveries. Guided by Faraday's experiments we can formulate the following law, which I shall call Faraday's Law of Flux Reaction:

The reaction of the flux at any point is determined by its density only. In vacuum and in certain material bodies it is equal to the flux density divided by a constant.

The reaction constant is called inductive capacity in the case of the electrical flux, and permeability in the case of the magnetic flux. Material bodies in which flux reaction is proportional to flux density will be called ideal bodies; the following discussion refers to them only.

The term "reaction of the flux," or briefly "flux reaction," requires a brief elucidation. Consider the picture of the tubes of force in an insulator; take a very narrow tube and imagine it cut up by planes perpendicular to it into volume elements of very short length. Each volume element will offer a small reacting force, the shorter the length of the volume element the smaller will be the reacting force. This is the reacting force of the tiny volume element. Divide it by the length of the volume element and the quotient is what is called here briefly "flux reaction." It is the reacting force per unit length of the flux. In a charged condenser the total reacting force of the flux along any curve from one plate of the condenser to the other is equal to the electromotive force of the charging battery, because the total reacting force of the flux and the acting force of the battery must, according to Newton's third law, be equal to each other and opposite in direction when the flux is in equilibrium.

Experiment shows that for ideal insulators the charge of the condenser, and, therefore, the total flux are proportional to the charging electromotive force. Hence with a given condenser the ratio of the charges, obtained with the same electromotive force, but employing two different insulators, is the same as the ratio of the inductive capacities. This is the ratio which supplied Faraday with a method of expressing the inductive capacity of solid and liquid insulators in terms of the inductive capacity of the vacuum which is the same as that of air.

Faraday's Law of Flux Reaction says nothing about the process which generated the flux; it must, therefore, be understood to express an emancipation of the fluxes from the processes which are responsible for their appearance; it does not matter whether they are due to charges or to the vortical forces discovered by Oersted and by Faraday. Their physical character as defined by their reaction is perfectly definite, no matter what their previous history is. In that sense they were an expression of Faraday's belief that electrical and magnetic fluxes are actually existing entities, manifesting themselves| through their reactions, which obey a definite law, the Law of Flux Reaction.

When an experiment succeeds in detecting and measuring the flux reactions at every point in space, and also demonstrates that they cannot be explained without the physical existence of Faraday's hypothetical fluxes, then the existence of the two new entities, the electrical and the magnetic flux, will have been nearly demonstrated. A complete demonstration demands, however, more than a knowledge of the flux reactions; if they are real entities they must be capable of action, also, and we must know how this action manifests itself. This brings us to the next step in Faraday's development of the flux concept.

FARADAY'S FOURTH AND FINAL STEP

When the external forces which generate the fluxes are equal at every point in space to the reactions of the fluxes at these points, then there is equilibrium and the fluxes remain constant. This is Faraday's physical theory relating to the equilibrium of the fluxes. At this point his theory was in the same state in which Galileo had found the science of statics, the science of Archimedes. Faraday's next step was the same as that which Galileo made when he began to study the motion of material bodies which are not in equilibrium. Faraday made that step when he framed an answer to the question: What happens when the fluxes are not in equilibrium? Aided by his experiments, which led him to the discovery of electromagnetic induction, he answered this question for the magnetic flux by formulating the fundamental law of electromagnetic induction as follows:

The electromotive force generated in a turn of conducting wire which is interlinked with a magnetic flux is equal to the time-rate of variation of that flux.

This law represents Faraday's magnetic flux as an acting entity; its action is measured by the generated electromotive force. I shall call it briefly Faraday's Law of Action. But observe that the action of the varying magnetic flux was detected and measured by Faraday in those parts of space only which contain the conductor.

It is opportune now to state the fundamental law of electromagnetism, first formulated by Ampère. For reasons which will be obvious presently I shall give it a form which employs a different terminology from that employed by Ampère himself. Since the electrical current in a conducting wire is always represented as a motion of electrical charges it can be also represented as a motion of the electrical flux which is attached to these charges. We can say, therefore, that the current is proportional to the time-rate of variation of the electrical flux which has passed through any cross-section of the conducting wire or through any area of which this cross-section is a part. The contour of this area is a curve which is interlinked with the conducting wire and with the moving electrical flux. With this understanding Ampère's fundamental law of electromagnetism can be stated as follows:

The magnetomotive force generated in a closed curve which is interlinked with the moving electrical flux of a conduction current is equal to the time-rate of variation of that flux.

Observe that the action of the varying electrical flux described here is that of the flux which is associated with moving charges of a conduction current. This law as worded represents Faraday's moving electrical flux as an acting entity; its action is measured by the generated magnetomotive force. I shall call it briefly Ampère's Law of Action.

The three laws, namely *Faraday's and Ampère's Laws of Action* and *Faraday's Law of Flux Reaction*, were the foundation of the electrical science which Maxwell inherited from Faraday. Since these laws are expressed in terms of the acting and of the reacting Faraday fluxes, these fluxes appear as the building-stones of that foundation. Upon this foundation of ideally simple construction the modern electrotechnical science was built. The concepts of the Faraday fluxes as represented in the formulation of these three fundamental laws were perfectly satisfactory to the electrical inventor and to the electrical engineer of Faraday's time, and even to those of our own day. Their achievements revealed a new physical reality, the reality of electricity in motion. It is not the whole physical reality which the electrical phenomena reveal to us to-day; the full meaning of Oersted's and Faraday's discoveries is unfolding rapidly, due to the great technical achievements of the *electrical science* which we inherited from these two discoveries. But as the reality revealed by electricity in motion unfolds we recognize more and more that Faraday's visions were not an empty dream.

These visions went much beyond the dynamo, the motor, the electrical telegraph, electroplating, and so forth; they never ceased asking: What is the connection, if any, between the activities of the fluxes and the activities of the forces which manifest themselves as light? Faraday knew that his science, the science of the electrical and of the magnetic fluxes, was still unable to answer this question, but that some day it would be. He had made four distinct steps in the development of the flux concept; he undoubtedly felt that at least one more step, the fifth step, was needed, but his experiments offered him no suggestion with regard to this fifth step. Experiment seemed to have reached a limit which even the resourcefulness of a Faraday could not pass.

Just as Galileo's experiments with freely falling bodies were the first step only in the creation of the modern science of dynamics of material bodies, so Faraday's experiments with moving and varying electrical and magnetic fluxes and the laws which these experiments formulated were the first efforts only in the creation of the modern science of flux dynamics. Newton completed the work which Galileo had started; it will be shown presently that Maxwell completed the work which Faraday had started. He discovered the fifth step which made the Faraday fluxes as real and as all-embracing as any concepts in physical science. We have good reason to believe that they are the cosmic bond of union between the countless parts of the visible universe, and that they carry the messages when, as the Russian poet Lyermontoff expressed it, "star speaketh to star."

IV

THE PHYSICAL REALITY OF ELECTRICAL RADIATION

FROM MAXWELL TO HERTZ

FARADAY was sixty-three years old when, in 1854, James Clerk Maxwell graduated with highest mathematical honors at Cambridge University. Maxwell was an alumnus of Trinity College, the alma mater of Newton. Faraday's researches became his favorite study as soon as he graduated; during his undergraduate days he had already started this study, and thus he enrolled very early as the first disciple of the great master. Personal contact with Faraday intensified the light which Maxwell had seen in his master's researches and in the visions which guided them. He made several efforts to reveal the meaning of Faraday's fluxes in terms of the language with which the mathematical physicists of those days were familiar. These efforts were deeply appreciated by his master, who, realizing that old age was rapidly approaching, was happy in the knowledge that in young Maxwell he had a brilliant disciple, to whom he could intrust the lighted torch which promised new revelations in the physical universe. In 1857 he said this in a letter addressed to Maxwell:

I hope this summer to make some experiments on the time of magnetic action . . . that may help the subject on. The time must be short as the time of light; but the greatness of the result, if affirmative, makes me not despair. Perhaps I had better have said nothing about it, for I am often long in realizing my intentions, and a failing memory is against me.

The inspiration which Maxwell received from these pathetic words can be seen in all of his efforts during the seven succeeding years. These efforts were finally crowned with a splendid victory when, in 1865, Maxwell announced to the world the completion of Faraday's theory of the electrical and magnetic fluxes. One can see in these efforts one supreme aim; it was to demonstrate that, as Faraday expressed it, "the time of magnetic action . . . must be short as the time of light." I never recall these words, without seeing in my imagination the picture of the aged philosopher, Faraday, passing to his young disciple, Maxwell, the lighted torch which was to reveal to mankind a new physical reality. What a glorious mission for a mere youth of twenty-six! But the youth was a poet by temperament, a keen and enthusiastic natural philosopher, a brilliant mathematician, and a man of a deep religious faith. The aged master saw these heavenly adornments of the soul of his young disciple; they were, undoubtedly, a great comfort to him in his declining years. The world is grateful that the aged philosopher, a "just and faithful knight of God," as Tyndall called him, was still living when his brilliant disciple delivered to the world the message which the master had been preparing by his epoch-making discoveries.

I cannot think of Maxwell's exalted mission without being reminded of Michelangelo's mission when he was appointed the chief architect of the uncompleted structure of Saint Peter's in Rome. Remodelling of the foundation and of the supports of its great dome, which he had designed and saw in his imagination, was Michelangelo's first problem. Similarly Maxwell's first problem was the remodelling of the foundation and of the supports

[102]

of the great intellectual dome which he had designed for the edifice of Faraday's science. He saw it in his imagination, and when he was ready to show it to others he wrote to a friend and said:

I have a paper afloat, with an electromagnetic theory of light, which, till I am convinced to the contrary, I hold to be great guns.

A very strong claim, made by the most modest of men! He could not help throwing off his usual reserve when he saw the beauty of the intellectual edifice with its glorious dome which was to be the monument to Faraday's immortal achievements.

MAXWELL'S RECONSTRUCTIVE EFFORTS

Faraday's Law of Flux Reaction, similar in form to the law of elastic reaction of an elastic solid, gave Maxwell the first suggestion for the solution of his problem. It told him that the energy of electrification and of magnetization is stored up in the fluxes themselves, a definite amount per unit volume at each point of the fluxes. The amount prescribed by the law of flux reaction was definite, and, in the case of vacuum and of what I called ideal material bodies, proportional to the product of the flux reaction and the flux density. This corollary of the law of flux reactions had never occurred to Faraday, because the Energy Principle had not yet become an infallible scientific doctrine when he first began to develop his concept of the fluxes. It could never occur to those who had paid small attention, only, to Faraday's hypothetical fluxes. The message of a prophet cannot be deciphered by the casual listener. To Maxwell the Energy Principle was one of the guiding lights, and he was not a casual listener. He had spent many a wakeful hour with Faraday's hypothetical fluxes and he believed in their reality.

Maxwell's localization of the flux energies in the volume elements of the fluxes gave to the fluxes a new claim to an actual physical existence. Their capacity of storing up energy presented to Maxwell a striking analogy to the storing up of elastic and kinetic energy in the volume elements of an elastic body. The elastic body became a visible picture of the fluxes. But the picture, though striking and most suggestive, was a deficient one, because the elastic and kinetic energy in the vol-

JAMES CLERK MAXWELL (1831–1879)
Discoverer of Electrical Radiation

ume elements of an elastic body are convertible
into each other. Faraday's and Ampère's fundamental laws of acting and reacting fluxes, as stated
above, did not exhibit a trace of convertibility;
that is to say, they indicated no means by which
the magnetic energy of a volume element can pass
from the magnetic flux of a volume element to its
electrical flux and vice versa. Without this convertibility there can be no transmission of energy
from volume elements to contiguous volume elements. This was the transmission which Faraday
advocated. Maxwell detected immediately that
the foundation of Faraday's theory of the flux
needed a reinforcement in this very spot, if it is to
demonstrate that the flux energies are transmitted
from point to point of the fluxes and with a definite velocity, perhaps equal to the velocity of light,
which was Faraday's vision. This demonstration
was Maxwell's great mission with which his master had intrusted him.

Maxwell solved his problem of reinforcing the
foundation of Faraday's theory of the fluxes by a
procedure the simplicity and effectiveness of which
were never surpassed in the history of physical

science. It can be described as a restatement of Ampère's and Faraday's Laws of Action in the following generalized forms:

The time-rate of variation of the electrical flux through any area is equal to the magnetomotive force in the circuit which forms the boundary curve of that area.

The time-rate of variation of the magnetic flux through any area is equal to the electromotive force in the circuit which forms the boundary curve of that area.

These two generalized forms of the fundamental laws of action I call Maxwell's Laws. They, together with Faraday's Law of the Reacting Flux, were employed by Maxwell as the reinforced foundation of Faraday's science. It would be difficult to imagine a simpler dynamical relation between the two fluxes, or to describe it by a more beautiful symmetry of expression. But Maxwell was a poet, and to him the laws of nature were just so many beautiful lines in the poem which the simple language of nature is addressing to the soul of man.

Maxwell's laws do not differ so much in form from Ampère's and from Faraday's Laws of Action as they do in substance. Here the difference is a fundamental one. In Ampère's Law of Action the flux variation is that due to the motion of the flux which is associated with the *conduction current*. Oersted discovered the magnetic forces produced by electrical conduction currents, and Ampère's law refers to these only. Maxwell's generalization of this law goes beyond experimental facts and assumes that any variation of an electrical flux passing through an area is an electrical current, *a displacement current*, through that area, and that, like the conduction current, it generates a magnetomotive force around the boundary of that area. That is to say, a varying or moving electrical flux in every volume element of space generates in that volume element and in its immediate neighborhood a magnetic force, and, therefore, a magnetic flux. This was the very thing which Maxwell needed.

In Faraday's Law of Action, on the other hand, the varying magnetic flux is represented as acting upon the electricities in a conducting wire by the electromotive force generated there. It says nothing about the action in those volume elements which do not conduct electricity. It was by the electrical conduction currents that Faraday had discovered the action of varying magnetic fluxes and had formulated his law accordingly. In his generalization Maxwell goes beyond the facts established by Faraday's experiments and assumes that wherever a magnetic flux through an area varies, it generates an electromotive force around the contour of that area irrespective of the substance in which that contour is located. If the substance is a conductor, then the generated electromotive force produces a conduction current; if it is an insulator, then the generated electromotive force will produce an electrical flux. That is to say, a varying magnetic flux generates an electrical flux; this, again, was just the thing which Maxwell needed.

Maxwell's generalizations were justifiable to the extent that his assumptions were justifiable. The following considerations show that the assumptions were justifiable as a heuristic attempt to penetrate deeper into the action of varying fluxes than Oersted's and Faraday's experiments had penetrated. If an electrical flux, which is associated with the moving charges of a conduction current, can generate a magnetic force, then why should not any other moving electrical flux produce the same result and in accordance with the same law? Besides, there is no sufficient reason to differentiate between the variation of an electrical flux through an area due to the motion of the flux through that area and that due to some other change. So much for the generalization in Maxwell's first law. Consider now the generalization presented in his second law. There is no inexorable reason to confine, as Faraday's experiments did, the action of a moving or varying magnetic flux to those parts of space only which contain conducting masses. Faraday did it because he had no means of detecting and measuring that action in the non-conducting parts of space.

Maxwell's reaching out beyond the limits of Oersted's and Faraday's experiments appears perfectly natural, when we remember that he believed the fluxes to be actual entities which not only react but also act in every part of space. A scientist does not display an unscientific mental attitude by going beyond known experimental facts and generalizing, provided that he makes justifiable assumptions and suggests a way of submitting them to experimental tests. The tools of the scientist are observation, experiment, and calculation. But this last tool, calculation, is not confined to extracting from known experimental facts all the logical consequences. A creative natural philosopher and mathematician, like Maxwell, cannot be limited to efforts of that kind; his intuition will not permit it, and a subtle intuition is one of the rarest gifts in science. Maxwell's poetic intuition saw in the elastic-body analogy a suggestion of additional attributes to Faraday's fluxes which they needed, in order to act as Faraday expected them to act. The suggestion was supported by his inimitable mathematical analysis. Faraday's and Ampère's Laws of Action in the Maxwellian form furnished these additional attributes.

Maxwell's generalized forms of the laws of flux action demanded that in every volume element of the fluxes the variation of one flux and of its associated energy generates the other flux and the energy associated with it. Here, then, is the convertibility of one form of flux energy into the other form in every volume element of the fluxes. This completed the analogy, first observed by Maxwell, between the activities of the Faraday fluxes and those of elastic solids. Hence the unavoidable inference that just as elastic solids transmit actions originating in any one of their parts to other parts with a definite velocity, so the Faraday fluxes must transmit the action from any one of their volume elements to other volume elements with a definite velocity. In elastic solids the velocity of transmission depends upon the reaction constants only, that is upon the elastic constant and the inertia constant, that is the density, of the elastic solid; similarly, the velocity of transmission through the Faraday fluxes depends upon the reaction constants of these fluxes only, that is upon their inductive capacity and permeability. The endowment of the fluxes with the power of acting and reacting, and with the capacity of storing two different forms of energy which are convertible one into the other, transformed them into media capable of transmitting their energies. These media have no attributes of ordinary matter as the luminiferous ether was supposed to have. They are ultra-material, but, nevertheless, they act and react with the same definiteness as an ordinary elastic solid. Our dynamical knowledge of a physical entity is complete when it can tell how that entity acts and reacts. If the laws of action and reaction of the Faraday fluxes are really those which Maxwell formulated, then the fluxes are dynamically just as real as the elastic solids are. It was this new glimpse of Faraday's ultra-material substances which encouraged Maxwell to make his bold assumptions. But the question arose: Are the assumptions and the laws to which they lead, Maxwell's Laws of Action, a correct statement of the actions and reactions of the Faraday fluxes? Experiment alone could answer that question.

As already stated, Maxwell's highest aim was to answer the question: How do the Faraday fluxes propagate their energy through space? His laws ofaction and Faraday's Law of Reaction answered this question; they led to a scheme of propagation very similar to the propagation of elastic and kinetic energy through a homogeneous elastic solid. This was to be expected on account of the analogy, mentioned above, which Maxwell had perfected. Maxwell's theory of propagation of the energy of Faraday fluxes showed, for instance, that in free space, that is in vacuum and in gases, like air, the velocity of propagation is the same as that of light. Moreover, the surface of the advancing fluxes, the so-called electromagnetic wave which carries these energies, is perpendicular to the direction of energy transference, the fluxes being in the plane of the wave and perpendicular to each other. This is called propagation by transverse waves. In other words, the wave of the fluxes, according to this novel and startling theory, has all the dynamical attributes of a wave of light. Hence Maxwell inferred that, in all probability, light is an electromagnetic phenomenon. This was the dream of Faraday.

But Maxwell's scheme of propagation was based upon a foundation which had two assumptions; without an experimental proof of the validity of these assumptions the theory, in spite of its beautiful simplicity and startling prophecy, could not stand. Maxwell said: "I have . . . an electromagnetic theory of light, which, till I am convinced to the contrary, I hold to be great guns." Experiment alone could bring that conviction. It is a remarkable historical fact that the obvious instrumentality for such an experiment was over a hundred years old when Maxwell wrote these memorable words. Franklin's Leyden-jar discharges were that instrumentality. Joseph Henry had experimented with them and proved them to be of an oscillatory character when Maxwell was still in his teens. Moreover, Joseph Henry suggested clearly that the electromagnetic action of Leyden-jar discharges was transmitted through space in a way which reminds one of the transmission of light. William Thompson, the late Lord Kelvin, who was, one might say, Maxwell's patron, friend, and scientific guide, had found the solution of the mathematical problem of oscillatory Leyden-jar discharges. This famous solution was published when young Maxwell, already a disciple of Faraday, was watching every philosophical hint which came from so great an authority as Thomson, of Glasgow, the theorist consulted by the promoters of the first Atlantic cable, the fairest ornament of Cambridge science in those days. No experimental researches in the electrical science stood in higher favor than oscillatory Leyden-jar discharges at the very time when Maxwell, inspired by Faraday, was pondering upon "the time of magnetic action." And yet neither Maxwell himself nor any one among his disciples ever suggested that oscillatory Leyden-jar discharges could be employed as an experimental test of the new theory of transmission of electrical and magnetic fluxes. It would make an interesting story to explain why Maxwell never attempted himself an experimental test of his theory with the aid of Leyden-jar discharges; but the story would lead much beyond the limits of this narrative. I must mention, however, that Maxwell's theory for many years after its publication had failed to convert anybody in Maxwell's native land to the extent of making him an enthusiastic disciple of the new electromagnetic theory of light.

The truth of the saying that no man is a prophet in his own land was never illustrated in a more striking manner than when Hertz, in Germany, published his experimental researches with Leyden-jar discharges. They demonstrated beyond all reasonable doubt that electrical and magnetic flux actions and reactions are transmitted through free space and through some insulators just as Maxwell's theory demanded. This happened twenty-two years after Maxwell's publication in 1865 of his immortal essay, "Dynamical Theory of the Electromagnetic Field."

Voltaire said that Newton's "Principia" was not "properly known" in France until forty years after its publication. He would have undoubtedly said that Maxwell's essay was not "properly known" in France or anywhere else until twenty-two years after its publication. The experimental researches of Hertz made it "properly known" everywhere. The world began to recognize then that Maxwell's essay is worthy to be placed alongside of Newton's immortal essay, and that they are the two greatest mathematical documents which revealed to the mind of man the existence of two distinct physical realities in the universe. One revealed the reality of matter in motion; the other revealed the reality of electrical radiation.

The Hertzian experiments are the foundation of the Radio art of to-day. No other technical art has a simpler foundation, and yet the vast majority of the users of radio receiving-sets look upon this art as a sort of magic. The transmission of sound appears to them a perfectly intelligible thing, because sound is a vibratory motion of air, and that, they admit, is a perfectly intelligible phenomenon. They do not admit that the transmission of the vibration of Faraday fluxes is also a perfectly intelligible thing, because they do not think that these fluxes are just as intelligible as air is. But they are; all that we know of air, as a carrier of sound energy, is that it is an elastic body which acts and reacts according to definite laws. We have the same knowledge of the Faraday fluxes; we know that they act and react according to definite laws. Air transmits the sound energy because it obeys the laws of action and of reaction of elastic bodies; the fluxes transmit the electromagnetic energy, because they obey the laws of action and of reaction of fluxes. Why, then, is one transmission a perfectly intelligible thing, and the other a magic? The reason is simple. In one case the transmitting medium is air, a material thing; in the other it is an ultra-material substance, a flux. The scientist does not hesitate to pin his faith on things which are ultra-material, like the Faraday fluxes, provided he knows their actions and reactions; the unscientific mind balks at making such a step. It cannot emancipate itself from the gross material world. A better knowledge of what is going on in energy transmissions which give us radio broadcasting will free the unscientific mind from its material chains, and prepare it for the understanding of the broadcasting of the heavenly stars.

THE HERTZIAN WAVES

It is opportune now to give a brief description of the most essential features of the Hertzian ex-

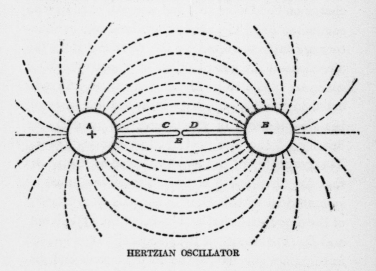

HERTZIAN OSCILLATOR

periments. They remind one of Franklin's Leyden-jar experiments; but Hertz, fully equipped with Maxwell's theory, employed a special form of a

Leyden jar, which radiates more abundantly waves
of Faraday's fluxes. It looks like a dumb-bell and
consists of two spheres, A and B, with projecting
rods C and D. A and C represent one conducting
plate of the jar, B and D represent the other; the
insulator between the two conducting plates was
air. Let an electrical machine generate a positive
charge on conductor AC, and a negative charge on
conductor BD. The charges on these two conductors are interconnected by the electrical flux; the
directions of the flux reactions at various points of
space are indicated by the dotted curves. As indicated in the diagram, they form tubular surfaces,
the cross-sections of which represent roughly the
density of the electrical flux at various points.
The symmetry of the apparatus makes it obvious
that the distribution of the electrical flux must be
symmetrical with respect to the axis of symmetry
of the apparatus, that is the axis of the cylinders C
and D. The energy of the electrical flux is located
in the space covered by the dotted curves and distributed in a perfectly symmetrical manner. The
release of this energy initiates the flux actions
which are to be transmitted. This release occurs as

follows: When the charge is sufficiently large, and, as a result the electrical force between C and D is sufficiently high, the reaction of the flux in the air-gap E breaks down and the air-gap becomes conductive. This releases the stored-up energy of the electrical flux, because the electrical charges on A and B move toward each other along the rods CD and the flux which is associated with them moves also. The energy of the electrical flux departs when the flux departs from the volume elements in which it was located; according to Maxwell's theory, it is transformed in every volume element of space into magnetic-flux energy. The disappearance of the electrical flux generates the magnetic flux, and it is a simple matter to form a picture of its location. In the immediate vicinity of the rods CD the curves of the magnetic flux must be interlinked with the rods and have a perfectly symmetrical distribution with respect to the axis of symmetry; that is, they are circular, the planes of the circles being perpendicular to this axis. At all other points of space they are also symmetrically distributed, and at each point in space the curves of the magnetic flux must be perpendicular to the curves of the electri-

cal flux. At every point in space there is, according
to Maxwell, a transmission of flux energy in the
direction which is perpendicular to the direction of
the electrical and of the magnetic flux. This transmission of energy is "electrical radiation." Hertz
demonstrated experimentally the existence of this
radiation; radio broadcasting is the offspring of this
demonstration.

How did Hertz demonstrate the existence of
electrical radiation which Maxwell's theory pre-
dicted? The answer is simple. If this radiation
exists and follows the laws of the propagation of
light, then in its passage from air to a dense material body it will be reflected. Hertz found that it
was partially reflected by the walls of his laboratory, and in order to make the reflection more complete he placed a conducting screen in the path of
the electrical radiation. Conductors, according to
Maxwell's theory, are opaque to electrical radiation, which is produced by rapidly varying electrical and magnetic fluxes, such as Hertz employed.
His Leyden jar, the Hertzian oscillator, was so designed that, according to Thomson's calculation,
mentioned above, its discharge was a vibratory

[121]

one, having a frequency, a pitch, of many million vibrations per second. The waves of electrical and of magnetic flux actions radiated by the Hertzian oscillator were, therefore, oscillatory, and when reflected by the metal screen the incoming waves and the reflected waves should form by interference standing waves; that is to say, according to Maxwell there should be in the path of the electrical radiation maxima and minima of the electrical and of the magnetic flux action. Hertz detected them and measured the distance between them. From the calculated frequency of the oscillatory fluxes and from the distance between the maxima or between the minima points the velocity was calculated. It was found to be about three hundred thousand kilometers per second. This velocity is the well-known velocity of light transmission. Hertz also found that the maxima of the electrical flux coincided with the minima of the magnetic flux, and vice versa; also, that at all points the electrical flux was perpendicular to the magnetic flux, and that the direction of propagation was perpendicular to both of them. This and several other experimental results were all in conformity with Maxwell's theory of the actions and of the reactions of electrical and of magnetic fluxes. The theory received its complete experimental verification.

These comparatively simple experiments proved the actual existence of the fluxes by the detection and measurement of their electrical and magnetic actions and reactions in various points of space. It is obvious that if there is an action in any part of space something must be there which acts; in the absence of material bodies some ultra-material substance must be there which acts. If that ultra-material substance acts and reacts in accordance with Maxwell's laws, as the Hertzian experiments demonstrated, then it has the attributes of Faraday's fluxes, and it is, therefore, dynamically represented by them.

It is an interesting historical fact that Hertz was born in the same year in which Faraday addressed his memorable letter to Maxwell, saying:

I hope this summer to make some experiments on the time of magnetic action. . . . The time must probably be short as the time of light. . . .

Maxwell caught a glimpse of Faraday's visions

which dictated that letter, and he embodied them into a beautiful physical theory. Hertz, thirty years after that letter was written, invented the experiments which translated those visions and the theory which they suggested into a simple physical reality, *the reality of electrical radiation.*

THE MOMENTUM OF MOVING ELECTRICAL FLUX

The revelation of electrical radiation made it highly probable that light is an electrical radiation. But the question arose: Does the oscillator which radiates light resemble the Hertzian oscillator? Hertz employed suitable loops of conducting wire, which he called resonators, for the purpose of detecting the electrical and magnetic actions in his electrical radiations. A second question, similar to the preceding one, arose, namely: Do material bodies detect the action of light by resonators resembling those which Hertz employed? The electrical science did not answer these questions until our knowledge of the structure of matter had sufficiently advanced. The pioneer step in this advance was made by Maxwell himself, when he formulated a new physical concept the existence of which was vaguely suggested by Faraday; it was the concept of the momentum of the moving electrical flux. Maxwell's conviction that Faraday's fluxes have a physical existence, that they are dynamical realities, suggested the question: Have they a momentum when they are in motion?

The momentum of a moving material body is the most fundamental physical concept in Newton's dynamics. It endows a material body with a power of action. Newton created the concept and it is one of his great achievements. Does not a similar power reside in a moving electrical flux? was Maxwell's question. One would expect Maxwell to formulate such a question. Did he not receive his earliest inspirations at Trinity College, in the atmosphere in which the spirit of Newton lived? Here Maxwell received the highest graduation honors, because he demonstrated that he had mastered Newton's science. Newton's momentum concept dominated Maxwell's dynamics. His own electromagnetic theory enabled Maxwell to answer his historical question completely; it is gratifying to know that a discovery made in this country was a great help in the formulation of this answer. The evolution of Maxwell's new physical concept, the momentum of the moving electrical flux, can be described briefly as follows:

If moving charges have a momentum in the sense in which moving material bodies have a momentum, then its change opposes a reaction against every action which produces that change. Our own Joseph Henry discovered, nearly a hundred years ago, that when he suddenly opened the circuit and interrupted the electrical current which sustained the magnetic flux of his powerful electromagnet, a large electromotive force was generated in the magnetizing coil. It produced an electrical arc in the air-gap where the circuit was opened. This is the so-called electromotive force of self-induction. If, following the terminology of Newton, this electromotive force be put equal to the time-rate of change of the momentum of the moving electrical charges, the so-called electrokinetic momentum, then this momentum receives a very simple physical meaning. According to Faraday's Law of Action, the electromotive force discovered by Henry is equal to the sum of the electromotive forces generated by the disappearing magnetic flux in the turns of the magnetizing coil. But the electromotive force in each turn is equal to the rate of change of the magnetic flux which is interlinked with it; call it the flux interlinkage of the turn. The electromotive force of self-induction is, therefore, equal to the rate of variation of the total flux interlinkages. Since this electromotive force was made equal to the rate of change of the electrokinetic momentum, it follows that this momentum is the same thing as the total flux interlinkages. This represents the momentum of the moving charges of Henry's magnetizing current by a simple graphical picture. It does not, however, display its intimate relation to the motion of the electrical charges which was Maxwell's aim. It is obtained as follows:

According to Oersted and Ampère, the magnetic force at any point in space produced by an electrical current is proportional to the current. Hence the magnetic-flux density in Henry's electromagnet and the total flux interlinkages of his magnetizing coil will be proportional to it. The electrokinetic momentum, which has just been proved to be the same thing as flux interlinkages, is, therefore, proportional to the current. This is the resemblance between the electrokinetic momentum of the moving charges of Henry's magnetizing current and the momentum of a moving material mass; this was Maxwell's aim. One is proportional to the electrical velocity, the current, and the other to the velocity of the moving material mass.

But the electrokinetic momentum just described is the momentum of the moving charges which constituted Henry's magnetizing current, and the reaction against its change has been considered in Henry's magnetizing coil only. Is this the only circuit where it manifests itself?

Maxwell's Law of Action of the magnetic flux says that the variation of the magnetic flux produces an electromotive force in all circuits, conducting as well as non-conducting. The electrokinetic momentum of Henry's magnetizing current and of every other electrical current, being the same thing as the magnetic flux generated by it, reacts, therefore, in all parts of space in the same way as it reacts in the circuit where the current flows; hence it exists in all parts of space where the magnetic flux exists. This becomes intelligible when, and only when, the motion of the electrical charges of a conduction current and of the electrical flux which is associated with these charges has a momentum in all parts of space where their flux is moving. It is obvious that every motion of an electrical flux must have a momentum irrespective of its being associated with moving charges of conduction current. This makes the magnetic flux in all parts of space the momentum of the moving or otherwise varying electrical flux.

The reduction of the magnetic flux to a momentum of the moving or otherwise varying electrical flux is intelligible in all cases in which we know that there is somewhere a variation of an electrical flux. But how about permanent magnets? Since the magnetic flux of permanent magnets acts in the same way as any other magnetic flux, we are forced to assume that it, too, is an electrokinetic momentum of unchangeable electrical currents in the atoms of permanent magnets. This assumption was first made by Ampère; Maxwell's concept of the momentum of the moving electrical flux makes Ampère's assumption a logical necessity. The electrical theory of matter which enjoys high favor today supports this assumption. Maxwell's electro-

magnetic theory reduces, therefore, all electromagnetic phenomena to the actions and reactions
of one primordial flux, the electrical flux. This reduction made Maxwell the Newton of the electrical
science, as will be seen in the following comparison.

Just as Newton reduced the science of matter in
motion to a few simple physical concepts, so Maxwell reduced the science of the electrical flux in
motion to a few simple physical concepts. The
momentum of moving matter is the fundamental
concept in Newton's science, the momentum of the
moving electrical flux is the fundamental concept
in Maxwell's science. Actions and reactions of a
material mass are the physical concepts which
Newton created; actions and reactions of the electrical flux are the physical concepts which Maxwell created. The fundamental laws in Newton's
science are similar in form to the fundamental laws
in Maxwell's science. In Newton's science these
laws describe actions and reactions of a material
mass; in Maxwell's science they describe the actions and reactions of the electrical flux. Newton's
science revealed a physical reality, material mass

[130]

in motion. The motion of the electrical flux revealed by Maxwell's science has an equal claim to be considered a physical reality, in spite of the fact that our ideas connected with this concept are apparently less concrete than those connected with our concept of ordinary matter. This concept is presented to our mind by our daily experience, the other concept is not.

But our ideas concerning the fundamental physical concepts are changing rapidly. The change produced by the influence of the radio art is a striking illustration. Every schoolboy who has constructed and operated a radio receiving-set understands the functions which his condensers, coils, and resistances have to perform. There are many, many boys in that class. They know that their condensers store the electrical flux and regulate its reaction, the capacity reaction, against a change of the quantity of the stored-up flux; that their coils are the guiding channels of the momentum of the moving flux and that they regulate its reaction, the inductance reaction, against a change of this momentum; that their resistances introduce a dissipation of the energy accompanying the motion of the flux, and that they regulate the dissipative reaction, the resistance reaction, which causes this dissipation. These young radio amateurs know by intuition, gained from thrilling experience with radio receiving-sets, that the capacity reaction is proportional to the quantity of flux stored up in the condenser; that the inductance reaction is proportional to the time-rate of change of the momentum of the moving flux; and that the resistance reaction is proportional to the velocity of the moving flux, that is to the electrical current. Later they will learn that the elastic reaction, the inertia reaction, and the dissipative reaction of a vibrating elastic solid follow laws which are identical in form with the laws of flux, just mentioned. They will say then that the behavior of the elastic solid is similar to the behavior of the electrical flux. The physical reality of the vibrating elastic solid will be revealed to them with the aid of the physical reality of the vibrating flux. The physical concepts of Newton's science will become intelligible to them when stated in terms of the physical concepts of Maxwell's science. These youngsters will probably be always more at home with electrical fluxes than with elastic bodies. They will see less magic in radio broadcasting than they see in the propagation of sound. Their descendants will probably see even less. This future *reformation of our mental attitude*, brought about by Faraday and Maxwell, will be just as great as the reformation of the mental attitude of the theologians brought about by the great scientific achievements of Galileo and Newton.

We all appreciate the great services of the radio art and of the telephonic art whenever we listen to words and music coming from a distance. We appreciate them even more when they place before us the speaking image of a distant friend. These are some of the audible and visible services of the modern electrical science. But there is an invisible service which this science performs and which is immeasurably greater, although it does not appeal to our senses directly. It is its service to the soul of man, aiding it to catch a glimpse of the ultra-material world, the world of the electrical flux, which transmits to us the language of nature from the remotest parts of the physical universe.

V

GRANULAR STRUCTURE OF ELECTRICITY AND OF RADIATION

The Hertzian experiments were a decisive demonstration that the Maxwellian theory of propagation of the electrical and magnetic flux actions and reactions was correct; that the waves of these fluxes are transmitted through free space, that is through vacuum and air, in accordance with the same laws as the waves of light. Maxwell's representation of the magnetic flux as the motion of the electrical flux simplified much his electromagnetic theory of light; if this theory is true, then light is a manifestation of the activity of only one primordial flux, the electrical flux. This was a close approach of the electromagnetic theory to the old ether theory of light, each of them demanding the activity of one substance only. But, nevertheless, the two theories had still a fundamental difference. The ether theory had to endow its ether with properties which were borrowed from

[134]

our knowledge of the properties of material bodies, namely elasticity and density. No experimental method was ever invented which could measure directly the elasticity and the density of ether. The ethereal substance started as a hypothesis and always remained a hypothesis. Besides, there were other insurmountable difficulties which need not be discussed here. On the other hand, the electrical flux did not remain a hypothetical substance; its physical existence manifested by its dynamical properties was demonstrated by Hertz beyond every reasonable doubt; these properties as defined by Maxwell's laws were not borrowed from the attributes of matter, as in the case of ether, but were derived from electrical experiments. Some day, perhaps, we might be able to describe the ether, if it actually exists, in terms of the actions and reactions of the electrical flux; today we do not need that description, in order to explain the transmission of radiant energy by transverse waves, progressing with the velocity of light. The actions and reactions of the electrical flux explain it satisfactorily for electrical radiation; there was always a hope that they would do it for the radiation called light, if light is in reality an electrical radiation.

The assumption that light is an electrical radiation, that it is a manifestation of the activity of the electrical flux, brought the electrical science face to face with two fundamental questions. Where is the origin of that flux activity? was the first question. By what instrumentality does ordinary matter respond to it? was the second question. The answer to the first question was obviously this: Material bodies are the origin of the flux activity, because they are the origin of light. The answer to the second question was less obvious. We could not say, fifty years ago, that material bodies respond in accordance with Maxwell's laws to the actions and reactions of the electrical flux which constitute light. Such an assertion would have gone much beyond experimental evidence, because these laws hold good for slow flux variations only, such as Oersted and Faraday had employed. Even the Hertzian oscillations were very slow in comparison with the enormous rapidity of variations which constitute light. Maxwell recognized this difficulty when he said:

Our theories of the structure of bodies must be much improved before we can deduce their optical from their electrical properties.

All experience encouraged the belief that electrical charges reside in material bodies; this belief was generally accepted, long before Maxwell had invented his electromagnetic theory of light. Since material bodies, being the origin of light, are the origin of flux activities which according to Maxwell's suggestions constitute light, the inference was permissible that these flux activities were associated with the electrical charges which reside in material bodies. Every advance in the electrical science since the discovery of electrolysis supplied fresh evidence that electrical charges, residing in material bodies, are granular in structure and that these granules are in all probability the centres of the electrical flux, the activity of which manifests itself as the radiation of light. A brief account of these advances was given in a popular address entitled "Ionization and Chemical Reactions," which I delivered last November before the New York Academy of Medicine. This is the address:

Ionization is a new word in physical science.

When I began to study physics forty-four years ago the word was not used in the college lecture-rooms. It was born thirty years ago and it is the offspring of the Roentgen-ray discovery. Behind this word there is a new science, the science of Electron Physics, which has been created during the last thirty years. In this new science we have a beautiful union between the sciences of physics and chemistry. I shall try to explain briefly one of the aspects of this union. A brief sketch of its history will, I think, prove useful as an introduction.

ELECTROLYTIC IONIZATION

The greatest scientific discovery of the nineteenth century is the discovery that light is an electromagnetic phenomenon. The glory of this discovery belongs to Michael Faraday, the Englishman, and to Clerk Maxwell, the Scotchman. It will forever be one of the greatest achievements of British science. According to Faraday and Maxwell, radiation of light originates in the activity of moving electricity. This means that in every radiating body there is a rapid motion of electricity,

[138]

so rapid, indeed, that its oscillations count many, many billions per second. One of the obvious pictures which this suggests to our mind is as follows: There is an electrical charge attached to the atoms and molecules of material bodies, and it must be very minute, otherwise it could not vibrate with the rapidity of the vibrations of light.

Franklin, nearly two hundred years ago, imagined that electricity had a minute granular structure, in order to explain the electrical current in a conductor. He represented it as the motion of tiny electrical granules through the interstices separating the conductor's atoms and molecules from each other. Franklin's intuition assumed a definite form when ninety years ago Faraday discovered that whenever a substance, say a salt solution, is decomposed by an electrical current a definite but very minute electrical charge is attached to each chemical valency of the decomposed molecules. This is the so-called Faraday law of electrolysis. The motion of these charges constitutes according to Faraday the electrical current through the electrolyte. Thus when water is decomposed into oxygen and hydrogen, then for each atom of oxygen there is twice as large a quantity of electricity set into motion as for each atom of hydrogen; oxygen has two valencies whereas hydrogen has only one. If in this decomposition the electrical charge moving with the oxygen is negative, then that transferred with hydrogen is positive and numerically equal to it. In the undecomposed molecule of water both charges are present in equal amounts and, therefore, they exert no external electrical force. But the internal electrical force between them may be very great, and it was believed to be by far the greatest force which acts between the components of a material molecule. The action of this force can and has been accurately measured in very many cases, and it is expressed in terms of the electromotive force which must be applied in order to produce a chemical decomposition of the molecule.

The greatest chemists of the early days of the nineteenth century, Berzelius and Sir Humphry Davy, expressed a belief that the electrical forces between the components of the molecule are the principal forces which guide chemical reactions. This belief was suggested to them by the discovery of electrolysis in the beginning of the nineteenth century. Faraday was a disciple of Sir Humphry Davy, and it is very suggestive indeed that his study of electrolysis furnished a powerful support to his teacher's scientific belief.

Faraday coined a new word, the word ion, the wanderer, and applied it to the carriers of electrical charges in electrolytic decomposition. Thus in the decomposition of water one component, the hydrogen atom, carries the positive charge in one direction and the other component, the hydroxyl, carries an equal negative charge in the opposite direction. The first is the positive and the second is the negative ion. Although it is not always possible to assign to each ion its definite chemical structure, it is always certain that in electrolytic decomposition these ions do exist and that their motion through the electrolyte constitutes the electrical current. Without this motion of the ions no continuous electrical current through any electrolytic solution is imaginable.

It was suggested by Clausius some sixty years ago that these ions exist in electrolytic solutions, even when no electrical force is acting, and that the presence of the electrical force directs only their motion, which manifests itself as the electrical current. Their existence, he believed, was due to the breaking-up of the molecules of the dissolved salt brought about by collisions accompanying that chaotic heat motion of molecules which manifests itself as temperature. This collision hypothesis concerning the generation of the ions was proved to be untenable, but their ever-present existence in electrolytic solutions was demonstrated in many different ways, particularly by measurements of the electrical conductivity of the solution, its osmotic pressure, rise of the boiling-point and lowering of the freezing-point. The experimental researches relating to this remarkable phenomenon, electrolytic dissociation, form the experimental basis of Modern Physical Chemistry, which may be said to have been born forty years ago. But its broad theoretical foundation was laid fifty years ago by Josiah Willard Gibbs, of Yale, whose work remained unknown in this country for nearly twenty years. It was also unknown in Germany when I was a student there. I discovered it by accident, and it supplied me forty years ago with material for a doctor's dissertation at the University of Berlin, and so I was the first to talk about him in Germany, and to eulogize him. I had good reasons to believe that these eulogies had made some impression, because three years later Professor Ostwald, of Leipzig, announced that he had just discovered Willard Gibbs.

Svante Arrhenius, the distinguished Swedish chemist, was the first to call the attention of the physicist and of the chemist to the remarkable difference in the physical and chemical behavior of solutions which conduct electricity and those which do not conduct it, as for instance a solution of sulphate of copper and a solution of sugar. The first is a conductor of electricity and is decomposed by an electrical current; hence it is called an electrolyte. The second does not conduct electricity, and, therefore, it cannot be decomposed by an electromotive force. Arrhenius was the first to explain clearly and convincingly this difference in the behaviors of electrolytic and non-electrolytic solutions by the assumption, first made by Clausius, that in an electrolytic solution the molecules of the salt are broken up into positive and negative

[143]

ions which in very dilute solutions act like independent molecules. The splendid experimental verifications of this assumption were so remarkable that no reasonable doubt could be entertained with regard to its correctness. This breaking-up of the salt molecules in an electrolytic solution was called, forty years ago, dissociation; to-day it is called ionization, this last name being more acceptable to the terminology of the modern electrical theory of atomic structure.

Some chemists of the old school objected to the idea of dissociation on somewhat curious grounds. One of them speaks of it in the latest volumes of the Encyclopædia Britannica as follows:

The war-cry of the molecules, according to Arrhenius, is: "We will dissociate, nothing shall prevent us." The chemist had more belief in the moral character of the molecules and expected that they would observe the marriage tie.

This venerable chemist is not aware of the historical fact that in the marriage ceremony which unites the components of a molecule there is no tie which was ever declared to be sacred and which nothing but death shall sever. The components of a molecule are partners only, with no sentimental bond between them except an agreement to engage in chemical business transactions which will be of mutual benefit. To illustrate: Consider a hydrochloric-acid molecule; it is a partnership between an atom of hydrogen and an atom of chlorine. A molecule of potash is a partnership between an atom of potassium and a molecule of hydroxyl. Dissolve them both in water and they will be dissociated into positive and negative ions, ready to engage in a chemical operation which actually takes place. A chemical reaction occurs, forming a molecule of water and two free ions, one an atom of potassium carrying a free positive charge, and the other an atom of chlorine carrying a free negative charge. They are an ionized molecule of chloride of potassium, ready and anxious for an opportunity to engage in a chemical reaction. This opportunity is given when, for instance, we drop into the solution some nitrate of silver. This is ionized and immediately its positive ion, silver, unites with the negative ion, chlorine, forming chloride of silver. The reaction is rapid, almost instantaneous, showing the great eagerness of the dissociated partners in the chloride of the potassium molecule to engage in a chemical business transaction. The transaction was made possible by the action of water, the solvent, ionizing each molecule into a positive and a negative ion. The ionization gives to the partners in a molecule a directing electrical force which enables their affinity to play its part when suitable opportunity is offered. Even the small number of opponents of some of the theories of the modern school of Physical Chemistry acknowledge that Arrhenius and his school of Physical Chemists did a splendid service to the science of chemistry when they established the close relationship between ionization in electrolytic solutions and their chemical activity. This is particularly true of ionization and chemical reactions which proceed with a high velocity.

This, broadly speaking, is a picture which guided Arrhenius and others in their successful efforts to establish a relation between ionization and chemical reactions. They furnished a splendid verification of the prophetic intuition of Berzelius, Sir Humphry Davy, and Faraday. Similar efforts have been made in other directions, and they finally led us to the electrical theory of matter. They gradually suggested a new view of chemical reactions which is an extension of the view first revealed forty years ago by the study of ionization in electrolytes.

IONIZATION OF GASES

Permit me now to give you a brief sketch of this advance in our knowledge of the atomic and molecular activity of matter. The path pursued by these efforts can be traced back to nearly forty years ago. It began when the earliest attempts were made to answer the question: Why do gases conduct electricity? We were accustomed to think that gases were ideal non-conductors. It was found, however, that bodies carrying an electrical charge will gradually lose it by leakage through the surrounding gas. The word leakage of electricity meant, of course, that the surrounding gas conducts electricity; badly, to be sure, but nevertheless it does conduct. Every schoolboy who ever watched an electroscope is familiar with electrical leakage, but forty years ago nobody suspected that the commonplace phenomenon, electrical leakage, would

[147]

some day unlock the door of a chamber which guarded many secrets relating to the electrical activity of atoms and molecules.

The first step in the advancement of this knowledge was made when it was found that electrical leakage can be greatly increased by the action of external agents, like ultra-violet light falling upon the surface of a charged body. The photoelectric cell, which plays a very important part in telegraphic transmission of pictures, is a very instructive illustration of this phenomenon. Guided by the theory of conductivity in electrolytes one was encouraged to imagine that the action of the ultra-violet light produces an ionization of the gas molecules, and that, just as in the case of electrolytes, this ionization is responsible for electrical conduction in gases. This guess was not a bad one, but it demanded an answer to a very perplexing question: How is the ionization produced by the action of ultra-violet light? Observe now that a completely satisfactory answer to the question, how is ionization produced in electrolytes, was never given.

The search for a satisfactory answer to the question, how is ionization produced in gases, resulted in the creation of the science of Electron Physics, one of the most beautiful creations in the history of science. Some future Homer in science will perhaps some day write an epic describing the wonderful adventures which scientific research, like an expedition into an unknown land, experienced on every step of its progress into the region of electrical conductivity of gases. The list of the heroes who played a glorious part in this expedition is as long as the list of heroes who found everlasting glory on the plains of Troy. But just as the name of Achilles rings in our ears whenever we hear Homer's Iliad mentioned, so the name of Thomson rings in my ears whenever ionization of gases is mentioned. This Thomson is Sir J. J. Thomson, Master of Trinity College, Cambridge, where immortal Newton composed his mathematical poem on *modern dynamics*, and where immortal Maxwell taught his electromagnetic theory to young J. J. Thomson, his successor in the chair of Physics at the University of Cambridge, and to-day Master of Trinity College, an honor much greater in many respects than to be the prime minister of England.

[149]

But pardon this digression; I forgot for a moment that my job this evening is to tell you a few things about "Ionization and Chemical Reactions" and not to recite poetry. But one cannot help losing control of his emotions whenever he contemplates the great scientific victories in the field of research relating to the electrical conductivity of gases.

ROENTGEN RAYS AND RADIO-ACTIVITY

Just as if imitating the method of procedure of the physical chemist who focussed his attention upon the conductivity of electrolytic solutions of high dilution, so the students of the electrical conductivity of gases focussed their attention upon the conductivity of gases at low pressures. This was illustrated thirty-five years ago by the great revival of interest in the phenomena of vacuum-tube discharges at extremely low gas pressures. The interest was rewarded by the discovery of the Roentgen rays thirty-one years ago. It was Thomson who first gave an experimental demonstration that the Roentgen rays are a radiation excited in the anode by the impact of small corpuscles moving with an enormous velocity and carrying tiny electrical charges of negative electricity from the negative to the positive electrode of the vacuum tube. Those who expected to find that these corpuscles were atoms carrying electrical charges which Faraday's law of electrolysis attaches to them were disappointed and puzzled. Thomson measured the ratio of this charge to the mass which carries them and found that this ratio is about eighteen hundred times as large as in the case of the smallest ion, the hydrogen ion. Nothing corresponding to that was ever found in electrolysis. Well, one was at liberty to imagine that Thomson's corpuscle was a tiny chip of an atom carrying a negative charge. Chip of an atom! Just think of it, who was bold enough in those days to imagine such a thing?

The discovery of radio-activity by Becquerel, thirty years ago, came to the rescue of the perplexed physicists. It was found that radio-active substances throw off positively as well as negatively charged corpuscles, the so-called alpha and beta rays, and also X-rays of great penetrativeness, called gamma rays in radio-activity. This discovery is one of the most remarkable discoveries ever

made by man. Just think of it, a bit of a radio-
active substance, say thorium, producing effects
with ease and grace, some of which Roentgen produced laboriously with huge induction coils and
most carefully exhausted vacuum tubes. The alpha
and the beta rays are deflected by the magnet, the
gamma rays are not. Employing Thomson's experimental method, it was found that the ratio of
the charge to the mass was the same for the negative corpuscles, the beta rays, as in the case of the
negative corpuscles of the vacuum tube, but for
the positive corpuscles, the alpha rays, the ratio
was smaller than that calculated for the hydrogen
ion in electrolytic decompositions. That meant
that the mass of the alpha corpuscles was larger
than that of the hydrogen ion. The physicist was
at liberty to imagine that the hydrogen ion is a
chip of the alpha corpuscle. The physicist was
puzzled more than ever, but in the course of a brief
period of time the puzzle was resolved. It was
found that the negative corpuscle was the same in
all cases and it received the name electron. Its
charge was accepted as the natural unit of negative electricity. The positive corpuscle correspond-

WILHELM KONRAD ROENTGEN (1845–1923)
Discoverer of X-rays, the foundation of Electron Physics

ing to the alpha rays was found to be a helium atom with a mass four times as large as that of the hydrogen atom. Finally vacuum-tube discharges revealed a positive corpuscle in which the ratio of the charge to the mass is the same as in the case of the hydrogen ion in electrolysis. It was found that its positive charge is numerically equal to the negative charge of the electron, and this became the natural unit for both electricities. It was also established by experiment that these corpuscles had no other mass except that due to their electro-magnetic energy, that is the energy attached to their charges, the mass of the positive corpuscle being nearly two thousand times as large as the mass of the electron, because its charge, although numerically equal to that of the electron, is nearly two thousand times as concentrated. The mass of the hydrogen atom, for instance, is that correspond-ing to the electrical energy of its electrical corpus-cles, that is, practically of its positive corpuscle.

Such were the discoveries which forced upon the physicist the theory that the atoms of matter are electrical structures, built up of negative and posi-tive corpuscles, of electrons and protons. The suggestion of this theory came from Sir Ernest Rutherford first, who to-day occupies the professorial chair occupied by immortal Maxwell fifty years ago. Thus according to Rutherford the hydrogen atom consists of a positive nucleus containing one proton, whereas a negative electron spins around it in orbital motion. The atom of helium has a positive nucleus, consisting of four protons cemented to each other by two electrons, and around this nucleus two electrons are moving in definite orbits, or, to be more accurate, the whole structure spins around its centre of gravity. Similarly every atom consists of a positive nucleus, which is made up of protons and electrons which bind the protons to each other and of orbital electrons spinning around the centre of gravity of the structure. In other words, each atom is a small solar system having a definite number of electronic satellites spinning with the central nucleus around the centre of gravity of the atom. The number of these orbital satellites is called the atomic number of the atom, and it is this number and not the atomic weight which determines the position of the atom in the Mendeleff series, thus determining its physical and chemical properties. According to this view of atomic structure, all atoms are multiples of the hydrogen atom, which thus becomes the fundamental structural unit in the material universe. The fact that the atomic weight of heavier atoms is not an exact multiple of the atomic weight of hydrogen is a remarkable fact, but instead of militating against the electrical theory of matter it is one of its strongest supports. The discussion, however, of this fundamental fact in the electrical theory would lead me too far.

But you will undoubtedly ask: What additional light does all this electrical theory of matter throw upon ionization and chemical reactions, which have been already described in connection with electrolytic ionization? A full answer to this question, though most interesting indeed, cannot be given in a brief address. The principal object of this lecture is to call your attention to certain phenomena which, I believe, are closely related to the science and art of the medical profession, and not to discuss them exhaustively. But one more point I must bring out as briefly and as clearly as I can. If the atoms persisted in that blessed state of beautifully co-ordinated orbital motion which I have just described to you there would be nothing of any importance to us going on in our stellar system. This stellar system would be a sleepy hollow in the universe, just as dead as the Sleepy Hollow cemetery at Tarrytown. There would be no light, no heat, no chemical reactions, and therefore no organic life of any kind anywhere. The persistence of that beautifully co-ordinated orbital motion in the atoms would represent a beautiful cosmos, but it would be a cosmos of death. The atomic and molecular activity in our stellar system is not a cosmos; it is a dynamic chaos, a greater chaos than that conceived by the liveliest imagination of ancient Greece. The electrical theory of matter as well as all our scientific knowledge demands such a chaos, in order to explain radiation, the most fundamental physical process in nature. To illustrate, consider the activity of a hot star, say our own sun. Its high temperature means that its atoms and molecules are in a state of violent and perfectly chaotic motion. Each atom rushes along just like a frenzied individual of a panicky mob. Billions and billions of collisions occur at every instant between the whirling atoms and at each collision orbital electrons are thrown out of their regular orbits. The serene atomic cosmos just referred to is smashed. During the return of the electrons from their temporary expulsion and exile the energy employed for their expulsion appears again as energy radiated out into space. Some of it reaches this earth, destined to sustain our terrestrial organic activity. Such is the activity of the life energy of the sun, that solar radiation may be described as the breath of life of the sun breathed into the nostrils of this terrestrial clay so that it may also live. But during the absence of the orbital electrons, expelled by the collisions, the atom is ionized; it is no longer electrically neutral; it is in a state similar to that of an ion in an electrolytic solution; it is electrically active. This type of ionization is not a mere fiction, invented to support the electrical theory of matter. The alpha, beta, gamma, and X-rays produce it in every gas and make the gas conductive. A charged electrometer placed in a gas chamber is universally employed to measure by the leakage of its charge the ionizing power of such rays. There are other ways of producing ionization of gases, and we understand to-day much better than we did forty years ago why ultra-violet light increases the leakage from an electrically charged body. Bold investigators like Millikan do not hesitate to employ most powerful forces in order to strip the atoms of most of their orbital electrons. In that state of extreme ionization the atoms display an intense eagerness to enter into chemical combinations, as if anxious to cover up as speedily as possible their atomic nakedness.

The ionization of the atoms is generally recognized as a stimulant for chemical actions, particularly those which proceed at high speeds. The function of the most powerful ionizing agents known to-day, that is the alpha, beta, gamma, and X-rays and ultra-violet light, becomes intelligible from this point of view. This point of view is in harmony with the electrical theory of matter, which endeavors to explain chemical reactions as due to the electrical activity of the atoms and molecules. Electrolytic ionization is one way of establishing this activity, atomic ionization is another. There may be many other ways. Who knows? The prophetic intuition of Berzelius, Sir Humphry Davy, and Michael Faraday, now a hundred years old, has been proved to be true. The forces of the electrical charges attached to the valencies of the atoms are the most powerful guides in chemical reactions.

SUMMARY

The wonderful advances of the electrical science enumerated in this brief sketch revealed an immeasurably wider view of Maxwell's electromagnetic theory than even a Faraday and a Maxwell ever dared to imagine. Guided by the prophecy of this theory, electrical research has drawn aside a giant curtain which like an impenetrable cosmic cloud had hidden from our view the electrical structure of creation, and it revealed a universe which baffles the imagination of the poet, the prophet, and even of the boldest speculative philosopher.

Maxwell's modest prophecy that light is an electrical activity is not only fulfilled, but we see that many other activities of matter are electrical activities; matter itself is a manifestation of electrons and protons, the converging centres of the electrical flux. There are no Hertzian oscillators in the

[159]

atomic structure of matter to start the radiating electrical waves, neither are there any Hertzian resonators to respond to the transmitted energy. These structural arrangements were the offspring of our experience with gross matter. We see now that the Hertzian waves were electrical waves radiated into space by countless legions of electronic centres moving as far as our gross senses could tell in unison, in perfect co-ordination. Maxwell's laws of electrical actions and reactions were founded upon our experience with co-ordinated motions of this kind. Franklin's Leyden-jar discharges and Volta's continuous electrical currents, which guided Oersted to his great discovery, were co-ordinated motions of electrical charges; so were the electrical motions generated by Faraday's electromagnetic induction. Our present knowledge of the granular structure of electricity shows that in all these cases the co-ordinated motion of the billions and billions of tiny electrons is a statistical average; that our observations, experiments, and calculations relating to electrical-flux activities were always dealing with averages. Maxwell's laws cover, therefore, the average activities, only, of the electronic centres. When we endeavor to pass from the average activity of an enormous number of electronic centres to the activity of each individual centre, then we enter a world where our ordinary physical concepts will probably not suffice. These concepts are the offspring of our gross senses; they must be amplified when we attempt to pass from the analysis of the average activity of an enormous number of individual actions to the analysis of the action of each individual. Our study of the radiation of light deals with the average activity of an enormous number of radiating centres. Our problem to-day is to express the average radiation of a given volume containing an enormous number of atoms in terms of the radiation of each individual atom. But Maxwell's theory says nothing about the electrical activity of an atom and cannot, therefore, give us any information about its electrical radiation. It finished its mission when it demonstrated that there are electrical radiations which in free space have all the characteristics of the waves of light, and when by that revelation it guided us to the revelation of the electrical structure of matter and to the radiations sent out by the tiny electrons which are the fundamental units of that structure. The electrical activity of the individual radiating units is entirely outside of the Maxwellian theory. A new experimental advance of the science of electrical radiations must be recorded before we can construct a satisfactory theory of radiation of the individual atom and its electrons. This theory must satisfy all our past experience with average radiations, that is, all our experience recorded in the science of spectrum analysis and in the empirical laws expressing a quantitative relation between the temperature of a body and its energy radiation. This is the field of electrical research which is as busy to-day as a bee-hive. Is there any honey? Yes, there is; some of it is sweeter than any honey that Mount Hymettus ever produced, and some of it is very bitter. For instance, our experimental records relating to the energy radiation of a body as a function of its temperature cannot be expressed by a satisfactory mathematical formula unless we assume that each individual atom radiates its energy in multiples of a very small but definite amount. The amount radiated is proportional to the vibrational frequency which is associated with that energy. This is, broadly speaking, the so-called Quantum scheme of radiation; it has received a splendid experimental verification and it represents *radiation as composed of tiny energy granules.* In order to construct an atom which will radiate that way, it is necessary to assign to the orbital electrons of the atom an activity which cannot be represented by any dynamical structure within human experience. This is an example of the bitter honey just mentioned. But the bees which made it tell us that the bitterness is all due to our untrained taste. *"De gustibus non est disputandum"* expresses a wisdom which was never more applicable than it is to-day in this embryonic period of the theory of electrical actions and reactions of the individual atoms and of its component electrons and protons. When that theory is completed it will certainly reveal new physical realities which may surpass all physical realities revealed so far to the expanding understanding of man.

It is well to mention here briefly the practical aspects of the preceding sketch of the Electrical Science.

The Cosmic Harness of Moving Electricity*

MOVING ELECTRICITY THE MOTHER OF ELECTRICAL ENGINEERING

The annual convention brings us together for the purpose of advancing our knowledge of each other and of the ideals of our society. We believe that our ideals are in harmony with the ideals of American science and American engineering, and, moreover, we believe that we have a place of honor among those whose mission is the cultivation and amplification of these ideals. They furnished the motive power for the rapid advancement of the science and the art of electrical engineering during the last hundred years. The advancement has been very rapid, but, nevertheless, no other art has a scientific foundation which is so deep, so broad, and so firm as the foundation of electrical engineering. In no other department of human knowledge are science and art so closely welded together. These statements, I know, many will consider as somewhat too bold. I shall try to justify them by

* President's address delivered at the annual convention of the American Institute of Electrical Engineers, June 22, 1926.

referring briefly to the outstanding events in the history of the art of electrical engineering and of the science to which it is welded.

• The very meaning of the word engineering implies an art which guides the activities of physical forces into channels of useful service. When the Galileo-Newton philosophy had disclosed the laws of motion of terrestrial as well as of celestial bodies, a new universe was revealed to man, a universe of orderly motion of matter in obedience to forces acting in accordance with laws of childlike simplicity. This philosophy suggested to the engineer new sources of power and service, and to the natural philosopher a new and apparently most comprehensive view of physical phenomena. Some philosophers, thrilled by the beauty of the new knowledge, believed that the whole future history of the universe could be foretold by the Galileo-Newton philosophy if we only knew at any given moment the configuration, the state of motion of every one of its parts, and of the forces acting between these parts. That was the mechanistic view of the physical universe which flourished soon after the triumph of Newton's great achievements. These achievements, however, misled some enthusiasts into the belief that all physical phenomena are reducible to orderly motions of matter under the action of gravitational forces. But as soon as man had discovered that other processes, not expressible in terms of motion of matter, formed an essential part of physical phenomena, that belief was abandoned.

Among these processes, the motion of electricity stands foremost. The new universe revealed by our knowledge of the motions of electricity appeals to our imagination so strongly to-day that many would not hesitate to rewrite the first sentence of the Book of Genesis as follows: "In the beginning God said, 'Let electricity move, and the embryo of the Universe began to form.'" Perhaps in a hundred years from now such a glorification of the motion of electricity will appear just as extravagant as the old mechanistic view of the physical universe. There is no doubt, however, that the nineteenth and the first quarter of the twentieth centuries will long be remembered as the epochs which revealed to us the hidden powers of electrical motions and their exalted position in our present knowledge of the universe. Who could have foretold all this when Stephen Gray, less than two hundred years ago, modestly announced that electricity can move any distance over conductors and that it does move with enormous rapidity? The world paid small attention to Gray's great discovery, and it might have continued its indifference if Franklin, instructed by his Leyden-jar discharges, had not inferred that lightning is a motion of electricity. Gray's modest terrestrial experiments received from Franklin a celestial illustration which commanded attention, although it was ridiculed by some learned members of the Royal Society. The motion of electricity which, in Gray's experiment, was detected by a tiny electroscope, assumed a sublime aspect when its flash in the heavens blinded the eye, deafened the ear, and shattered many stable structures of man.

Franklin's discovery of the electrical character of lightning was a great stimulus to the study of the motion of electricity. One may compare it to the stimulus which the Copernicus-Kepler revelation concerning the motion of the planets gave to Galileo's study of the motions of terrestrial bodies.

Just as Copernicus and Kepler gave us a Galileo and a Newton, so Gray and Franklin were destined to be succeeded by an Oersted and a Faraday. But it required a Volta to introduce Oersted; it required large electrical motions to reveal the magnetic forces of moving electricity which Oersted discovered.

Prior to Oersted, the engineer moved material bodies and guided their motions into channels of useful service by providing a material connection between the driving and the driven body. Oersted showed that a material body which is the seat of electrical motions can make other bodies move without a material connection between them. The magnetic flux is the invisible coupling. Oersted's discovery of the magnetic field which accompanies electrical motions promised, therefore, to give birth to a new type of engineering, employing a new type of coupling. This promise was one of the great incentives to the advancement of the new knowledge. The mechanical action of an electrically charged body upon other bodies gave a similar promise, but it failed, and it was destined to fail to make that promise good. The promise of the Oersted discovery blossomed out into a reality more beautiful than the fairest dream which prompted that promise. Electricity in motion offered to the engineer a moving force which proved much more powerful than that offered by electricity at rest. The lifting power of Henry's electromagnets was immeasurably greater than the lifting power of the gravitational action of the material out of which his electromagnets were made. One can imagine to-day what an impression that new fact must have made upon the mind of the engineer of a hundred years ago. To-day one can say that electrical engineering is the science and the art which tell us how to make material bodies move by employing an invisible harness hitching up these bodies to moving electricity. It was born when Oersted made his discovery, but its growth was destined to be slow as long as the Voltaic battery was the only powerful means of generating and sustaining electrical motions. To Faraday belongs the glory of discovering a new and much more powerful instrument than the Voltaic battery. It was his clear vision which prophesied a reciprocal relation between moving electricity and moving magnetism.

The prophecy was probably the offspring of the intuition which suggested that since moving electricity moves magnets, it is reasonable to expect that moving magnets will move electricity. Faraday discovered that this expectation is correct, and he offered to the engineer an ideally simple and powerful method of setting electricity in motion. The promise of Oersted's discovery to the engineer assumed a new meaning after Faraday's discovery, and electrical engineering began its career which placed it in the exalted position it has to-day among the engineering sciences. The efforts of the electrical engineer to render useful service by hitching up material bodies to moving electricity resulted in the creation of the dynamo, the motor, the transformer, the telegraph, the telephone, and other epoch-making devices which have revolutionized the material conditions of human life. Grateful mankind responded with a generous support of the science which gave birth to and nursed the young art of electrical engineering and, like a wise mother, gave it its exalted ideals. These ideals are the bond of union between electrical engineering of to-day and its trusty guide, the electrical science. The progress of one brings quickly an equal progress of the other, because hand in hand they always walk together with equal step. One cannot contemplate their stately walk without recalling to mind the well-known line from one of the odes of Horace:

"O matre pulchra, filia pulchrior!"

THE HARNESS OF MOVING ELECTRICITY

The enormous lifting power of electromagnets was the great scientific sensation of a hundred years ago. It excited the lively imagination of Joseph Henry, at that time a young engineer, and he was the first to give it a novel service when he designed the first electromagnetic telegraph which gave the first real job to the electrical engineer of a hundred years ago. The enormous lifting power of the electromagnet furnished also a new job to the natural philosopher when it forced upon him the question: What is the invisible coupling through which this force is transmitted from the stationary to the movable part of the electromagnet? Faraday was the first to suggest an answer to this question. His discoveries and visions detected what

[171]

one may call an invisible electromagnetic harness
to which all material bodies in the universe are attached and which is always available to be employed by moving electricity in useful service.
Faraday and Maxwell taught us that this harness
is woven out of the electrical and magnetic tubes
of force. Change the electrical elements of this cosmic harness in any part of space and its magnetic
elements will also be changed in accordance with
Maxwell's extension of Ampère's law. Change its
magnetic elements and its electrical elements will
be changed in accordance with Maxwell's extension
of Faraday's law of electromagnetic induction. It
is by these changes that an action is transmitted
from one part of free space to another. A more
complete, and, at the same time, ideally simple description of the operation of the invisible harness
than that given by Maxwell was unthinkable sixty-
one years ago. It became the foundation of the
electrical science as well as of the electrical art, that
is of electrical engineering; it welded the two to
each other. Faraday and Maxwell performed the
welding process. Their mode of thought appealed
to the engineer because it expressed the motion of

energy from one part of space to another in terms of the action of the invisible coupling between them, furnished by the tubes of force. No elaborate mathematical process was required to aid our understanding of this action, and yet the Faraday-Maxwell electromagnetic theory was often accused of being too mathematical, because its fundamental laws, mentioned above, when expressed mathematically were called Maxwell's equations. This conveyed the idea that the theory is a mathematical apparatus which cannot be operated by the mathematical skill of an ordinary electrical engineer and is therefore of no use to him. Nothing can be more erroneous than this notion. Nothing is more concrete and simple than the Faraday-Maxwell electric and magnetic flux and nothing is more extensively used by the electrical engineer than these fluxes and the simple laws which govern their activity. No elaborate mathematical apparatus is necessary in order to understand that the Faraday-Maxwell science revealed to us the most accurate understanding of not only the mode of operation of the invisible coupling in ordinary electrical-power generation and transmission, but also in the transmission of radiant energy from the distant stars to our terrestrial globe. This understanding gave us the first glimpse of that unity of the universe in which the invisible harness, joining every one of its parts to every other part, is always ready to transmit service which moving electricity makes available.

Faraday and Maxwell, however, had not spoken the last word concerning the invisible cosmic coupling. New explorers of the boundless region, revealed by the visions of Faraday and Maxwell, have delivered and are still delivering new messages from this region, unfolding many of its secrets. What are these secrets and how does their unfolding affect the views of the electrical science and its art, electrical engineering?

Franklin was the first to profess the belief that all electricity has its origin in material bodies. Faraday's discovery, that to each atomic valency there is attached a definite electrical charge, gave Franklin's belief a more intelligible form, which appealed to our imagination more and more as the conviction grew stronger that all chemical reactions are due to the activities of the atomic charges.

It was this conviction which suggested the name "electron" to the smallest unit of atomic charges long before its independent individual existence had been demonstrated by actual experiment. Roentgen's discovery of the X-ray suggested the hypothesis that these rays are excited by the impact upon the anode of tiny projectiles, shot forth with enormous velocities from the cathode of a high-vacuum tube. Experiment proved that these projectiles are the individual electrons, the existence of which in the atomic structure had been suggested by Faraday's electrochemical discoveries; experiment also determined their electrical charge and inertia. This is the foundation of modern *Electron Physics*, and it is so broad that it furnishes new support to the foundation of the Faraday-Maxwell electromagnetic theory, to chemistry, astrophysics, meteorology, biology, and, above all, to electrical engineering. It has created a new electrical industry and a new type of electrical engineering. It is the busy electron in the amplifying vacuum tube which gives life to the radio broadcasting industry and supplies new problems to the electrical engineer, the so-called radio engineer; it carried conviction to those who were inclined to think that the tiny electron was only a fiction of a supersensitive imagination.

THE ELECTRON, THE PRIMORDIAL UNIT OF POWER GENERATION

The marvellous success of this new electrical industry and of the electrical engineering which guides it, directed our attention to the function of the electron in all electrical-power operations. The result is that to-day the electron and its positive partner, the proton, have become the fundamental concepts in the science of modern physics and in the art of electrical engineering. The tubes of electrical force between them are the primordial electrical flux, the fundamental and the only substance in the web of the cosmic harness. The relative motion of that primordial flux manifests itself as the magnetic flux which measures the momentum of this relative motion. Relative to what? Relative to the observer who is measuring that momentum. A charge moving with the observer has no momentum relative to the observer and is not accompanied by a magnetic field which the observer can detect.

Electron Physics made a fundamental contribution to the achievements of Oersted, Faraday, and Maxwell when it demonstrated the individual existence of the electron and the proton and pointed out that the electrical flux, which unites the two, is the primordial flux, the cosmic bond of union between all electronic granules in the universe. This is the invisible harness to which all parts of the cosmic space are hitched up. To the electrical engineer who is a disciple of the Faraday school of thought the electronic granules are unintelligible except as local convergencies of the primordial flux. It is the activity of the flux which tells him the story of energy movement from one part of space to another, and without this energy transferrence the motion of the isolated electronic granules would have but a very small interest for him. He is, it is true, interested in the cosmic processes by which heavier atoms are evolved out of lighter atoms by a suitable grouping of the electronic granules, but that which interests him incomparably more is the energy liberation in these processes

and the invisible harness along which the liberated
energy is transmitted, destined to perform some
useful service in some distant part of space. He is
also interested in the energy which is stored up in
the formation of the atomic nucleus, and how much
of it can be made available when the structure of
the nucleus is changed as in radio-activity.

Electron Physics interpreted in terms of Faraday's visions and Maxwell's quantitative formulation of them suggests to the electrical engineer a
universe which reminds him of a power-distribu-
tion system in which there are an endless number
of power-stations all interconnected by the primordial flux. Material bodies, from the smallest atoms
to the biggest stars, are, according to this picture
of the universe, local aggregations of electronic centres in the all-embracing, primordial flux. This
cosmic structure, however, is not a static but a
dynamic one. Every one of its electronic centres is
in a state of activity, receiving energy from its
busy neighbors and giving it out without cessation
or rest. It is pulled by or is pulling at the cosmic
harness to which it is inseparably attached. It is
doing its share of service in the evolving universe,

[178]

and how much of this service is to benefit man depends upon the man himself; upon his science and art of electrical engineering. It is the problem of the electrical engineer to transform the activity of the infinitely numerous, but infinitely small, electronic toilers in the cosmic power-stations into orderly service for the uplift of the life of man. He is the co-ordinator of the restless activity of these toilers; they follow his bidding as if guided by the magic wand which Faraday and Maxwell and their disciples gave him; they are obedient servants. Here they heat an electrical furnace and there they guide chemical reactions; here they drive the propellers of a battleship, and there they turn the busy wheels of an industrial plant; here they speedily carry the weary industrial toiler to his home and there they make it cosey and comfortable by their light-giving service; here they record the cheerless figures of the stock-exchange ticker, and there they carry sweet melodies and soul-stirring language to the millions of eager listeners on this hopeful continent.

It is a master mind, indeed, that can thus control the activity of an infinitely numerous army of toilers. No vulgar rule of the thumb can find a lasting place in the logic of such a mind; its art is an exact science and its science is supported by an art the experience of which, through many generations, has been tested by methods of measurement of astronomical precision. No vague and hazy notions obscure the lucidity of the electrical engineer's operations. The enormous electrical efforts of his million-kilowatt power-station are just as lucid to him as the feeble efforts of the tiny electrical power which brings us the wireless message from distant Australia. Both of these efforts are huge in comparison with the efforts of a single electronic toiler in terms of which the electrical engineer can express every electrical effort. He knows the numerical value of the labor of these tiny workers and he also knows that it is their toil by which the lily, without toiling or spinning, arrays itself in beauty which far surpasses Solomon in all his glory. It is their toil which promises to the civilization of man a beauty and glory which will far surpass the beauty of the lily. The mission of the electrical engineer is to make this promise good. In the performance of this mission he will keep always in mind the following words of the Holy Scriptures:

[180]

And seek not ye what ye shall eat, or what ye shall drink, neither be ye of doubtful mind.

But rather seek ye the kingdom of God; and all these things shall be added unto you.

The men who made the science and the art of electrical engineering did not seek what they should eat or drink. But in their thirst and hunger for the eternal truth they did seek and find, in part at least, the kingdom of God, which resides in the beauty of their science and its art, and in the beauty of the universe which they reveal. That science and its art are the creation of a new philosophy which we call the philosophy of idealism in science. It is the simplest philosophy ever constructed by the mind of man and represents the essence of scientific experience of centuries; an experience which was always guided by a definite motive, a definite mental attitude, and a definite method of work. The motive was the unselfish longing for God's eternal truth; the mental attitude always demanded an open-minded and unprejudiced interpretation of nature's language; the method of work is that by which our patron saints Gray, Franklin, Volta, Oersted, Ampère, Faraday, Maxwell, Roentgen, and their disciples created the science and the art of electrical engineering. This motive, mental attitude, and method of work is the firmest foundation of the scientific idealism which is the idealism of our profession, and we have always been the leaders in the propagation of its gospel. We were the earliest apostles who converted the American industries, so that to-day they worship at the altar of the Idealism of Science. We must impress that idealism upon all phases of our national life, in order to assist our nation in the solution of the many complex problems of modern democracy.

FROM CHAOS TO COSMOS*

THE LAW AND ORDER OF THE MACROCOSM

THE history of civilization reveals several epochs which witnessed remarkable changes in man's views of the physical universe. Modern science takes no deep interest in those views which resulted from poetic intuition or from purely speculative thought, but were not suggested by scientific observation, experiment, and calculation. Hence the views concerning the universe formulated during the epochs preceding the birth of modern science offer little interest to the student who believes that these views have no intrinsic value unless they are permissible suggestions of scientific knowledge. If we adopt this standard of measure, then the views of the universe based upon the ancient atomic theories of Democritus and of Lucretius or upon the ancient doctrine of continuous flux in the

* Suggested by the author's first Josiah Willard Gibbs lecture delivered before the American Mathematical Society.

existence of all things advanced by Heraclitus have no intrinsic value, because they have no background of scientific knowledge. The earliest view of the universe which merits attention according to this standard is the view which was suggested by astronomy, the first among modern sciences which adopted and developed the true scientific method, the method of observation, experiment, and calculation. This view will be considered first.

The most inspiring sight ever beheld by the human eye is the starry vault of heaven. "The firmament," says the Psalmist, "sheweth His handiwork." The stars in the firmament were, to the Psalmist, the visible parts of an ideally perfect structure which presented to man's inquiring mind the first visible picture of the unchangeable, the eternal; this picture encouraged him in the belief that high above the eternal stars resides an immortal divinity. Hence the ancient belief among Indo-Europeans that after death the immortal soul of man rises along the milky way to its divine abode above the stars.

Man always turned his eyes to the stars when

[184]

he sought knowledge and inspiration. There he found his earliest physical concepts, which now form the language of modern science. His earliest knowledge of dynamical laws was a reward for his long-continued efforts to understand the motions of the heavenly bodies. The names of Copernicus, Kepler, Galileo, and Newton will forever remind us that the oldest of physical sciences, the science of dynamics, was revealed to us by the unchangeable planetary orbits. Two centuries elapsed before the puzzle of these orbits, born and nursed in the minds of Copernicus, Kepler, and Galileo, was finally resolved by the genius of Newton. No story ever told by man surpasses in beauty Newton's story of planetary motions, and none was ever told in fewer words. If brevity is the soul of wit, then Newton's story entitled "Philosophiæ Naturalis Principia Mathematica" is the acme of human wit. The orbit of our earth around the sun, and the resultant recurrence of the terrestrial seasons, succeeding each other with a rhythm which has not changed perceptibly within the record of human history, are revealed here as the result of an unchangeable law of action between material bodies.

One often wonders which is the more beautiful, this ideally simple law, the law of gravitational action between material bodies, discovered by Newton, or the simplicity of language with which he states it. The power of mathematics never was more glorified than in Newton's symbolic statement of this law and of its far-reaching consequences. Its symbols gave us the power of prophets; they enabled us to predict the future state of motion of any member of the planetary system from the state of motion of that system at a given time. To predict by a comparatively simple calculation from an ideally simple law the moment of arrival of an eclipse, with an accuracy measured by a tiny fraction of a second, is indeed a wonderful achievement. That kind of motion is a splendid illustration of what the Greeks called *Cosmos;* that is, a creation of law and order, in contradistinction to *Chaos*, which denoted to the Greek mind a shapeless mass devoid of all intelligible law and order.

I shall employ here the words *co-ordination* and *non-co-ordination* to describe the conditions which the Greeks called cosmos and chaos. It was, then, the perfect co-ordination in the motions of the heavenly bodies as they appeared to the Psalmist which inspired his words:

> "The heavens declare the glory of God;
> And the firmament showeth his handiwork."

It was certainly the beautiful co-ordination in His handiwork which inspired Copernicus, Kepler, Galileo, and Newton to search for its hidden cause. Newton's law of action between material bodies revealed the secret. One cannot help feeling that our idea of perfect co-ordination, of an ideal physical cosmos, is of celestial origin, and that it was Newton's genius which brought it down to earth, and made it a part of human understanding. The science of dynamics which Newton created may be called the dynamics of *co-ordination*, and with this understanding we can say that modern science rests upon a foundation of *co-ordination*. This foundation is therefore a cosmos, a beautiful creation of law and order.

The beauty of Newton's discovery, and its startling revelations, gave birth to the eighteenth-century hope that some day all physical phenomena might prove themselves reducible to some kind of co-ordinated motion of matter. That hope was strengthened by the study of co-ordinated electrical motions. From Stephen Gray, a contemporary of Newton, who had started this study, to great Faraday and his equally great pupil, Maxwell, there is a time interval as long as that which separated Copernicus from Newton. The achievement in each one of these time intervals was equally great; no other time interval of three hundred years in human history can boast of an equal intellectual achievement.

Maxwell's formulation of the fundamental laws of electrical motions is the greatest intellectual achievement of the nineteenth century. It was surprisingly similar to that which Newton gave us in his "Principia" concerning the motions of matter, and it exhibits the same simplicity and power of the language of mathematics. Nothing could be simpler than Maxwell's language, which, in a few and simple mathematical symbols, revealed a new truth perhaps even more startling than Newton's law of gravitational action. This new truth is: Light is an activity of electrical forces, generated in the interior of luminous bodies and propagated through all space in accordance with the funda-

mental laws of electrical motions which he had
formulated. The agreement of this new doctrine
with experiment was as startling as the agreement
of planetary motions with Newton's laws of action
between material bodies. One should never look
upon the starlit vault of heaven without remember-
ing that it inspired not only Newton but also Maxwell in their revelation of a new and more complete
interpretation of the Psalmist's words:

"The firmament showeth his handiwork."

It is an interpretation which says that the laws of
action of matter upon matter produce the ideal co-
ordination in the motion of the planets and of the
other material bodies in the heavens as well as on
the earth, and that the laws of action of electricity
enable the stars to send to us by their electrical
activity the light messages which help us to observe, understand, and admire the beautiful co-
ordination, the cosmos, of celestial motions. A
more complete analysis of the beauty of law and
order in the co-ordinated physical world was never
given by mortal man. It is a splendid outcome of
long-continued efforts of the human intellect during a period of nearly four hundred years.

This historical sketch of the scientific achievements of the Newtonian school may be called a sketch of the first part of the cosmic drama, which suggested to the human mind a picture of a co-ordinated universe. It gave strength to the belief that all physical phenomena would some day be explained as co-ordinated motions of matter and of electricity. This belief was an offspring of the ancient belief that this world was a chaos in the beginning, and that some day it would be a cosmos, a beautiful creation of law and order. This, indeed, would have been the simplest and the most intelligible world; the human mind loves the beauty of simplicity, probably because where there is simplicity there is intelligibility. But a new knowledge, which saw the light of day less than one hundred years ago, gradually developed new physical concepts which made that belief untenable.

We know to-day that co-ordinated changes in the state of physical bodies can explain a small part only of physical phenomena, and that the non-co-ordinated changes in the physical universe are vastly more numerous. The beautiful co-ordination in the motion of a star, and Newton's analysis of it, were certainly most inspiring, but new sciences have been born since Newton's time which teach us that co-ordinated motions can tell us an infinitesimal part, only, of the story of stellar and of terrestrial activity.

THE CHAOS OF THE MICROCOSM

The disciples of the school of co-ordinated motions studied the motions of matter and of electricity in the *macrocosm*, in the large-scale world, in which we observe directly the motions of the stars and planets in the heavens, of the seas and clouds and of other terrestrial objects. But in the beginning of the nineteenth century science began to catch the view of a new world, called the *microcosm*. The revelations of the microcosm form the *second* part of the cosmic drama.

The study of the activities of material bodies forced us to recognize that both matter and electricity are granular in structure, and not uniform, as our coarse senses had led us to believe. The activity of matter and of electricity in the macrocosm is, and we should expect it to be, different from the activity of their component granules, the vanishingly small but almost infinitely numerous

its study marked the beginning of a new science, not, like Newton's science of dynamics, inspired by the beautifully co-ordinated motions of celestial bodies, but of a most humble origin. It was born in the musty boiler-room, but it grew heavenward, until to-day its noble head touches the stars of heaven.

CARNOT'S LAW

The first great achievement of the new science is barely a hundred years old, and it was an achievement of Sadi Carnot, the great French engineer and scientist of Napoleonic times. He gave us the fundamental law of action of the moving power of heat, or, as he called it, "the moving power of fire." His teacher was the steam-engine, and his law is a law of efficiency which tells us how to get the most service from a given quantity of harnessed heat energy by the operation of a steam-engine or of any other caloric co-ordinator. It was a startlingly novel method of expressing what proved to be a fundamental physical law in terms of the efficiency of a mechanism invented by man. It seemed to be devoid of the æsthetic beauty and of the philosoph-

[194]

ical rigor of Newton's laws, the operations of which were not tied to any specific human invention. The hidden beauty and philosophic significance of Carnot's law have been revealed gradually by scientific research during the last hundred years.

"Hitch your wagon to a star" and you will certainly get somewhere is the promise of Emerson. But if you should hitch your wagon to a molecule, which in its motion collides incessantly with other molecules and therefore changes its schedule a countless number of times during every brief moment of its erratic history, you will get nowhere. If, however, you hitch your wagon to a steam-engine, the piston of which is driven by the bombardment of a countless number of erratic molecules of the boiling fluid, Carnot's law will predict with mathematical accuracy the path of the co-ordinated motion of your vehicle. The piston averages up the erratic molecular pulses, producing a steady pressure. This supplies the driving power of the steam-engine and of the machinery which is coupled to it.

Just as the steam-engine co-ordinates the non-co-ordinated activity of the erratic molecules of the hot steam, so the galvanic cell is a co-ordinator of the non-co-ordinated chemical activity of the atoms and molecules of the metals and fluids in the cell. It produces in conductors a co-ordinated motion of the non-co-ordinated granules of electricity, the electrons, which are thus enabled to serve us in any of their many co-ordinated modes of motion, like driving a motor, or electroplating. The action of a dynamo is another form of electrical co-ordination, and there are many other electrical co-ordinators, revealed by the discoveries of the Faraday-Maxwell period. The co-ordinator is a concept which is foreign to Newtonian dynamics. It is, according to the illustrations given above, a mechanism which connects the world of non-co-ordinated to that of co-ordinated activities, the microcosm to the macrocosm. Carnot's law of efficiency is the simplest description of the law of operation of a caloric co-ordinator.

CARNOT'S LAW APPLIED TO CHEMICAL REACTIONS BY GIBBS

The gradual generalization and extension of Carnot's law made it evident, however, that it was not, as appeared at first, merely a convenient efficiency rule for the power engineer, but that it had a deeper philosophical meaning. No man among the early investigators gave this law a more generalized meaning than did Josiah Willard Gibbs, our American physicist and illustrious scientist of Yale. He may be called the Newton of chemical and caloric dynamics, the dynamics of non-coordination. Gibbs was the first to give us a mathematical method by which we can calculate in any system of chemical reactions that part of the non-co-ordinated chemical energy which is available for co-ordinated external service.

Even the splendid work of Gibbs, however, did not hide the fact that the dynamics of non-coordination was born in the musty boiler-room, and that its fundamental law was primarily an answer to an apparently sordid question, the principal question of the boiler-room: How much service can a man get out of a ton of coal?

This apparent taint of materialism in Carnot's law encouraged the view among some academicians of the early period that the starry vault of heaven was the exclusive abode of the cosmos of co-ordinated physical phenomena, and that the chaos of non-co-ordination and its science were to be found only on our imperfect terrestrial globe. This view was excusable a hundred years ago; but to-day, thanks to the labors of Willard Gibbs and of others, and to the discovery of spectrum analysis, we have a much broader view of the non-co-ordinated physical processes and of the laws governing them. Not the earth, but the stars, are recognized as the real seat of non-co-ordinated energy. We know that the chaotic activity of the molecules of hot terrestrial bodies is a feeble illustration, only, of the behavior of the molecules in a luminous star such as our sun. A very great, probably the greatest, part of the stellar energy is stored up in heat, the energy of non-co-ordinated motion of stellar molecules and atoms. The most complete picture of a chaos is our mental image of the non-co-ordinated motion of the molecules and atoms of a young, white-hot star. Here we find a restless chaos of violent molecular collisions which are the primordial source of cosmic energy. The most striking illustration of prodigality is the lavishness with which radiation pours out into space the life energy of such a star. Nothing in this lavishness suggests the sordid question: How much of this non-co-ordinated energy is destined to be harnessed, and how much useful service will be gained from the harnessed stellar radiation? Efficiency and waste are concepts taken from the vocabulary of human experience of toil. They are unknown in the vocabulary of the luminous stars. A realization of the enormous energy capacity of these cosmic furnaces and of the lavishness of expenditure of their activity makes one feel the omnipotence of the Creator and of his power to keep these furnaces alive forever.

The question of the service which non-co-ordinated stellar energy can render is a terrestrial one. It was first suggested by another question, namely: What is the terrestrial mission of solar radiation? The very formulation of this question implies that man always recognized the dependence of life upon solar radiation. This involves dragging anthropomorphism into science. But what of it? Science stripped of all its human elements would become inhuman. Considerations of the human element in science reveal to the human soul the full beauty of science. It is the consideration of the human element, which, in my opinion, gives to the dynamics of non-co-ordination a beauty and charm which otherwise would not be found there. I venture to point out some of these elements by considering briefly the function of several terrestrial co-ordinators which are not, like the steam-engine and the galvanic cell, inventions of man, but structural attributes of inorganic and organic matter.

INORGANIC AND ORGANIC CO-ORDINATORS

Carnot and Gibbs tell us how much of the radiated non-co-ordinated energy of the sun is available for the performance of co-ordinated service, provided there is a co-ordinator of solar energy. Every thoughtful student of Carnot and of Gibbs understands that the blessings of a summer shower which are carried to the parched lips of thirsty earth are due to the transformation of a part of the non-co-ordinated solar energy, radiated to the waters of our earth, into co-ordinated motion of water vapor. The instrumentality for this transformation resides in the molecular structure of water. This is the co-ordinator which makes the great and glorious sun in the heavens work like a faithful servant for the humble peasant on little earth by turning the busy water-wheel of his mill. Carnot and Gibbs and their dynamics of non-co-ordination formulated the law of its operation.

A similar instrumentality, residing in the cellular structure of plants, enables the same solar power to sustain the life on earth by the transformation of a part of its radiant energy into co-ordinated growth of plants and of animals. That sunlight makes plants grow is a fact the knowledge of which is as old as human history, but the efforts to recognize in that fact a special case of a general physical law were first made by the philosophers who followed in the footsteps of Carnot and of Gibbs. The more closely we examine plant life on the earth the more we become convinced that one of the principal objects of this life is to catch the non-co-ordinated radiant energy of the sun and transform it into co-ordinated activities on the earth, the transformation of the energy of the celestial chaos into co-ordinated terrestrial service. They are co-ordinators; they transform the resplendent sun-god, the golden Helios of classical Greece, into a willing servant, a fireman, of tiny earth. Without this service there would be a speedy end to all terrestrial life. Ancient sun-worship testifies that the value of this service to man was recognized several thousand years ago by the poets of Rig-Veda and Mahabharata, when the human race was young, and science had not yet been born. To-day our knowledge of the fundamental law in accordance with which this service is rendered gives additional force to our praise of Him from whom all blessings come. It adds another element to the interpretation of the Psalmist's words: "The firmament sheweth His handiwork." Who can say when that interpretation will be complete? Certainly not until the fountain of revelations in science runs dry.

Our earth, through its organic and inorganic structures, co-ordinates the non-co-ordinated radiant energies which are transmitted to it, and makes them obedient servants in the support of earth's living organisms. These co-ordinators obey the same fundamental law which the co-ordinating action of a steam-engine obeys. But it is in this

JOSIAH WILLARD GIBBS (1839–1903)
Father of Physical Chemistry

respect only that the co-ordinating action of terrestrial organisms, like that of the leaves of plants, resembles the action of a steam-engine. Beyond that the similarity ceases, because the details of their modes of operation are different.

One of the differences I shall briefly describe. Most of us are familiar with the selectivity of the radio-receiving instruments. It enables us to select any one from innumerable messages that may be passing through space in any chaotic fashion. We pick out that message the wave-length of which is in resonance, that is in tune, with our receiving apparatus. Maxwell taught us long ago that the radiant energy of the sun reaches us as electrical waves. Mathematics tells us that the material structures on the earth receive and harness it, principally because the molecular elements of these structures resonate electrically to some particular wave-length of the innumerable electrical waves transmitted to us by myriads of solar atoms. This transmission process is non-co-ordinated, because each solar atom is an essentially independent station for broadcasting its own share of the solar radiant energy. When the reactions of our terrestrial atoms are in tune with the actions of solar atoms which transmit the waves, then the interaction between the two may be described as being due to a sympathetic responsiveness, called electrical resonance. Here, then, is a harmonious relationship between our terrestrial globe and the stars of heaven, the existence of which appeals to our imagination, because of its similarity to harmonious human relationships. Neither the Psalmist of old, nor Copernicus, Kepler, Galileo, and Newton in more recent times, ever suspected its existence. The poets may have dreamed about it. We know it to-day, and this knowledge gives additional meaning to the Psalmist's words of praise of the firmament, the handiwork of God.

The contemplation of apparently commonplace terrestrial operations, first suggested by the humble steam-engine, leads us back to the stars, our first source of inspiration, which gave us the laws of material co-ordination in the motion of the material macrocosm. We appeal to the stars again for guidance in our attempts to interpret broadly the meaning of the laws of non-co-ordination. We return to them by a path which at first seemed to move along apparently sordid terrestrial ways, like questions of the efficiency of transformation of the chaotic energy of steam into co-ordinated service. The path leads from the musty boiler-room on little earth to the glorious stars in the boundless heaven.

Truth is beautiful and divine, no matter how humble its origin; it is the same in the musty boiler-room as it is in the glorious stars of heaven. From the non-co-ordinated molecular activity of the fire under the boiler to the co-ordinating activity of the steam-engine there is a progressive advance which reveals the same universal truth, as the progress from the non-co-ordinated solar activity to the co-ordinating activity of organic structures on earth. The steam-engine gives life to the machinery in our busy factories, the co-ordination of solar activity gives life to our terrestrial organisms. In each case, so far considered, the object of co-ordination is to rise to a higher level in the scheme of creation by rendering service. It is the call for service which transfers the chaotic activity of the stellar microcosm to the co-ordinated activities of the terrestrial macrocosm. Carnot's law of efficiency loses its taint of materialism when we look at it from this point of view.

SERVICE, THE ULTIMATE PURPOSE OF CO-ORDINATORS

It is the introduction of anthropomorphism into science which gives to Carnot's law of efficiency of the operation of a caloric engine a broader meaning by attaching to it the broader idea of service. This idea in its most general aspect is very helpful when one attempts to interpret the meaning of those operations by means of which the chaotic activity of the microcosm of the external world is transformed into the co-ordinated cosmos which we call organic life.

The full meaning of organic life is still a mystery and it will probably remain a mystery until this terrestrial globe has added many æons to its already advanced old age. The physical foundation of life, however, is no longer a deep mystery. The beauty of its material structure and of the operations of this structure will, in my opinion, be much more obvious when we look at it from the point of view of dynamics of non-co-ordination.

If in a figurative sense we call every physical activity life, then every radiating atom has life, and even this most elementary concept of life continued to be a deep mystery from the very beginning when

God said, Let there be light; and there was light.

To-day this mystery is not as deep; we believe that we have resolved it, partly, at least. How did physical science proceed in its study of this primordial concept of what I call here the life of the atom? The answer is simple. Following a brilliant suggestion of Sir Ernest Rutherford, it painted a picture of the structure of the atom, and then endowed the elements of that structure with certain modes of motion which constitute the life of the atom. A brief inspection of Rutherford's picture is opportune now.

The physicists are fairly confident that the components of the atomic structure are an equal number of positive and negative electrons. The positive electrons are cemented together by the attractive force of a certain number of negative electrons and form the central positive nucleus of the atom.

The remaining negative electrons move in elliptic orbits around the central nucleus. Each atom is thus represented by a structure which is pictorially a faithful copy of a solar system; it is a cosmos, a creation of law and order. But whereas the members of our solar system have not changed their co-ordinated motions within the memory of human history, the orbital motions of the negative satellites in the atoms experience innumerable changes during each tiniest interval of time, due to collisions with neighboring atoms. Each collision throws out one or several orbital electrons from one of their stable orbits to another. It is during these jumps, only, from one stable orbit to another, that the energy of the atom is radiated into space; nothing happens while the orbital satellite moves in the same stable orbit. The satellite in its stable orbit is dead as far as the outside world is concerned; and if not dead it is certainly fast asleep. A collision of the atom with its neighbors wakes it up. If all the orbital electrons in the sun and in the luminous stars should persist in their motion along the same stable orbits without occasionally jumping from one stable orbit to another, the world would return to the condition which is described in Genesis in the words

And the earth was without form, and void; and darkness was upon the face of the deep.

The words of Genesis,

And God said, Let there be light; and there was light,

mean, therefore, in our present picture of the atom and its radiating activity that "in the beginning" the orbital electrons were waked up by the collisions of the chaotic motions of the atoms, and jumped from one stable orbit to another. There is a never-ending struggle going on between chaos and cosmos in the life of atoms; without this struggle the atoms would be sleepy hollows, as dead to the outside world as a cemetery.

Whenever I think of the radiating activity of the orbital electrons in the sun I am reminded of the clapper of the bell in the church spire of my native village. If it had not been for the activity of that clapper I should have slept through many an early mass on Sundays and holy days, particularly in winter, when blessed sleep in a warm bed seemed to me so much more heavenly than acting, long before sunrise, as an •acolyte in the wintry atmosphere of a cold village church. The busy orbital electrons in our luminous stars are the atomic clappers which send the call of the stars into the ear of slumbering matter on earth: Wake up from your idle slumber; live and serve in this beautiful temple of the Creator!

No physicist believes that this picture of the atom and of its activity is a faithful and finished portrait of this primordial unit of cosmic energy. It is an ideal picture, but the imagination which painted it was guided by all our knowledge of the activity of the invisible original. In the same manner science has painted a picture of the physical foundation of organic life. We know that in all probability it is not a very close likeness to the original and that it is in fact an unfinished picture, but we believe that every new stroke of the brush which science will add to it will make the picture more and more true to the original. Dynamics of non-co-ordination will help to add these strokes. Carnot and his most distinguished pupil, Willard Gibbs, will guide the brush.

CARNOT'S PRINCIPLE*

Introduction by the presiding officer, William F. Durand, Ph.D., LL.D., president of the American Society of Mechanical Engineers:

I have spoken of Sadi Carnot as a great Scientist-Engineer; by this I mean that while he ever burned with zeal in the discovery of new and hitherto unknown truths, he was, at the same time, always alive to their useful application in the service of humanity. And so, in seeking for a speaker to open for you in more detailed measure the pages of the life and work of Carnot, what more appropriate choice could your committee have made than that of a man of the same type, a man who, by a long life rich in scientific achievement and always alive to the significance of the useful application of science to the needs of humanity, has exemplified the highest and finest ideals of the Scientist and of the Engineer? A man again who, by both written and spoken word, has interpreted to students of the modern age the thoughts of the great man whose memory we honor on this occasion. Such a man they have found. I have very great pleasure in introducing as the next speaker Doctor Michael I. Pupin, of Columbia University.

* An address delivered at the Carnot Centenary Commemoration before the United Engineering Societies on December 4, 1924.

One hundred years ago a principle was discovered which marked the beginning of a new era, not only in the history of science but also in the history of all human thought. Its great discoverer was Nicolas Leonard Sadi Carnot, and hence the name Carnot's Principle. The fame of the discoverer has never passed beyond the boundaries of a comparatively small circle of scientists and engineers. This may seem strange, but it is not as strange as the historical fact that it took fully twenty-six years before that discovery could find its way even into the tiny circle of the foremost scientists of Europe. The reasons for this delay of recognition are not far to seek.

Carnot's Principle, as originally formulated by the discoverer, is the only trusty guide in our studies of the operations by which heat is harnessed to do mechanical work and render service during its passage from a higher to a lower temperature level, an operation so well illustrated by the performance of the steam-engine. But in order that heat may perform that service it is necessary to guide it in its passage from higher to lower temperature levels by a suitable mechanism, and Carnot described an ideal mechanism by means of which the maximum service is obtainable. Carnot was only a youngster of barely twenty-eight, and wholly unknown to the academicians of France, when in 1824 he published his epoch-making essay "On the Moving Power of Fire." The concepts of "work and energy," so clearly defined in Carnot's mind, had only just begun to find their way into scientific thought, so that as we look back to-day we cannot help thinking that Carnot was far ahead of his time; he was a prophet, and a prophet is always hard to understand. Hence the long delay of recognition; it came nearly twenty years after Carnot's death in 1832, when he was only thirty-six years of age.

The prophet differs from the ordinary man by the intensity of the impressions which the environment makes upon his mind. He is a man of emotion and inspiration. What inspiration guided Carnot in his prophetic thoughts? Was it the operation of the steam-engine, and nothing else? I do not think so, but even if it had been so, then another question would arise, the question, namely, What inspiration guided the inventor of the steam-engine? I shall now touch upon a subject so well discussed last Tuesday by Doctor Low, the retiring president of the American Society of Mechanical Engineers.

We recognize to-day that there is, as Doctor Low said, a cosmic stream of solar energy from which everything that lives and breathes on this terrestrial globe derives its driving-force, just as the mill on the mountainside derives its driving-power from the mountain stream. This cosmic stream of energy is the mighty flow of solar radiation. The oceans catch it and derive from it the lifting-power of their vaporous water-masses, which, driven by atmospheric currents, distribute their precious loads over the thirsty continents. Countless billions of drops of water are thus carried by solar radiation to the highest continental elevations, and before they return to the oceans again each one of them has performed a definite mission. No relief expedition has ever performed a more precious service to terrestrial life than these tiny messengers of our terrestrial oceans are performing continuously. If science could find a Homer who would describe in suitable language the adventures of some of these drops of water on their cyclic journeys from the oceans to the continents and back again, the world would read an epic alongside of which Homer's "Odyssey" would sound like a commonplace tale. This Homer of science has not yet been found, although five thousand years ago the poets of Rig-Veda and of Mahabharata told us that in those days man's mind saw in this solar energy stream and in the service which it rendered to terrestrial life a new divinity, and founded a religion of solar worship. This was the result of the ancient inspiration.

Contrast now with this ancient mind the modern mind of the inventor of the steam-engine. Where one saw the resplendent sun-god, the other saw a celestial fire and imitated it by a terrestrial fire under a boiler. Where one saw the blessings of the sun-god, manifesting themselves in the healthy growth of terrestrial life, the other saw evaporation of the oceans and the gigantic mechanism which lifts the enormous water-masses destined to irrigate the continents; he imitated it by providing the boiler of the steam-engine which by the pressure of its steam drives the piston of the steam-engine and does work which relieves man of the heaviest burdens of physical labor. The cosmic operation, as well as its tiny terrestrial imitation, the steam-engine, employs the same cyclic process of harnessing heat in its passage from higher to lower temperature levels for the purpose of making it serve man just as the mountain stream in its downward course serves the happy miller on the peaceful mountainside. But neither the ancient sun-worshipper nor the modern inventor of the steam-engine knew anything about the fundamental law in accordance with which heat performs this precious service to man. The revelation of this simple truth was reserved for a prophet who had the vision to see a new truth in physical phenomena which had become commonplace, because from time immemorial they surrounded us on every side and all the time.

Now what is the fundamental truth which Carnot extracted from the familiar phenomena which accompany solar radiation and the operations of a steam-engine?

The first part of this truth was an axiom, and it is this: "Heat cannot perform mechanical work except when it passes from a higher to a lower temperature level." Carnot illustrates this axiom by pointing out that, similarly, water stored in a reservoir cannot do external work except when it passes from its own to a lower level.

Wherever, therefore, there is a difference of temperature levels there is an opportunity of harnessing heat for useful service during its passage from the higher to the lower temperature level. The blessings conferred upon our terrestrial globe by solar radiation have undoubtedly helped to suggest to Carnot this self-evident truth. The axiom itself cannot fail to remind us that there are billions and billions of blazing stars whose temperature levels above the surrounding space are much higher than that of the sun, and are, therefore, capable, each of them, of rendering similar service and to a similar extent as the sun. The sight of the stars should therefore remind us that there are in the physical universe inexhaustible stores of opportunities for rendering service similar to the service which solar radiation is rendering to our terrestrial globe. With this axiom in our mind we shall always find the word "service" written across the starry vault of heaven. When the Psalmist sings

The heavens declare the glory of God,

remember that in this declaration the word "service" is the biggest word.

It is a matter of universal experience that direct conduction of heat from a hot body to a cold body in contact with it will produce no other effect than to raise the temperature of one and lower that of the other. No mechanical work is done under these conditions, and, therefore, no service is rendered which forms the subject of Carnot's philosophy. That kind of heat-transferrence is a waste of opportunity, according to Carnot. When, however, we interpose a suitable instrumentality in the path of heat which is being transferred, then service may be rendered. This is what we call harnessing of heat. The piston in the cylinder of the steam-engine is such an instrumentality, it is a part of the harness. The steam in the cylinder expands and drives the piston against external pressure and thus performs work at the expense of a part of the heat of the steam, the other part passing on to the condenser. The steam-engine with its well-known cyclic operations is a crude illustration, only, of what Carnot meant by an instrumentality which enables heat to render service during its passage from a higher to a lower temperature level. Carnot himself described a much more perfect instrumentality for these cyclic operations; it is a steam-engine idealized in its construction as well as in its mode of operation by expansion and compression.

It is not necessary to go into any detailed description of Carnot's poetic conception shown in his ideal engine and its ideal cyclic operations, except to say that they are reversible. The scientific meaning of this term, first employed by Carnot, is best described by the statement that whatever changes occur during the cycle when it is performed in one direction will be reversed when the cycle is performed in the opposite direction. This is to say, if during a cycle of expansions and compressions heat is passed from a higher to a lower temperature level and a certain amount of work is delivered by Carnot's engine, then when the cycle is reversed the same amount of work delivered to the engine will transfer to the higher temperature level the same amount of heat, otherwise a *perpetuum mobile* would be possible, and that, following the Newtonian dynamics, Carnot rejects as impossible. Carnot shows then by the simplest kind of logic ever employed by a scientific mind that under these ideal conditions the maximum amount of mechanical work is obtained by the passage of a given quantity of heat from a given higher to a given lower temperature level, and that this maximum depends upon the initial and the final temperature, and upon nothing else. This is Carnot's Principle. It can, therefore, be summed up briefly as follows:

Heat can do mechanical work by passing from a higher to a lower temperature level, if suitably harnessed. When that passage is effected by means of a reversible cycle, the maximum amount of work will be obtained, and this amount will be independent of everything except the initial and the final temperature.

Twenty-six years elapsed before the full importance of this principle was clearly understood. Young William Thomson, who later became Lord Kelvin, but who at that time was only twenty-six years of age, was the first to decipher Carnot's message, and this enabled him to construct a new and absolute scale of temperature. It was then an

[220]

easy matter to express Carnot's Principle in the various mathematical forms known to-day as the Second Law of Thermodynamics.

The first advance upon Carnot's work was the result of many efforts, notably those of the great Maxwell, to explain dynamically the efficiency of the transformation of heat into mechanical work, as demanded by the second law of thermodynamics. The first result of these efforts was the confirmation of an old belief that heat is a non-co-ordinated mode of molecular motion. This was vaguely suggested by many scientists of the eighteenth century.

The molecular motion in a hot gas offers the simplest illustration. We call that motion non-co-ordinated, because each molecule, being practically an independent unit, performs its motion according to its own sweet will, colliding incessantly with its neighbors. It is a chaotic state of motion, and we can say that among the enormous number of molecules contained in a cubic foot of hot gas there is a chaotic distribution of kinetic energy. The function, then, of Carnot's piston is to receive the impulses due to this chaotic mode of motion and to transform them into a co-ordinated form of motion of the machinery connected to the piston. This is, indeed, a transformation of a chaos into a cosmos, and the highest efficiency obtainable by man is that given by Carnot's Principle.

The chemical energy of a finite mass is also distributed among an enormous number of atoms. When these atoms unite in a perfectly unrestrained way, we have again a chaotic distribution of activity, each atom jumping, so to speak, in an unrestrained way into the arms of the atom with which it unites and generating heat, just as a weight freely falling to the ground will generate heat by impact. But, as was pointed out by Thomson over seventy years ago, when a Galvanic cell is the seat of chemical reactions and as a result of them external work is done by employing the generated motion of electricity to drive a motor, then the dissipation of chemical energy into heat may be very greatly reduced. The Galvanic cell may, therefore, be called a co-ordinator of the chemical activity in the same sense in which that name has been applied to the function of the Carnot piston. This indicates roughly how Carnot's Principle has found its way into the study of chemical reactions so beautifully worked out by Josiah Willard Gibbs, of Yale.

The co-ordinating action of the Voltaic cell has been in the mind of many an investigator when he made the efforts to guide the chemical reaction between oxygen and carbon by the co-ordinating action of Voltaic forces.

Permit me to refer again, briefly, to Doctor Low's inspired remarks on Tuesday last. I refer now to his sketch of the process of storing solar energy by the biological activity of the plant cell. This energy is radiated by myriads and myriads of solar atoms and molecules, which are practically independent of each other. Their activity is, therefore, chaotic, and the energy units which they contribute to the mighty stream of solar radiation form a non-co-ordinated system of energy distribution. The action of this chaotic system upon the plant cell is similar to the action of steam molecules upon the piston. The result of this chaotic action is a perfectly co-ordinated separation of oxygen from carbon in the carbon dioxide absorbed by the leaves from the atmosphere; it leads to a co-ordinated form of mechanical work as the growth of the plant testifies. It is a beautiful transformation of a chaos into a cosmos, a beauty of order. Each plant is a cosmos, a part of which is derived from the chaos of solar radiation. This action of the plant cell is, as Doctor Low says, still a secret. We can describe it briefly by saying that the plant cell has co-ordinators which, like the Voltaic cell and Carnot's engine, guide chaotic activity into coordinated forms of service. This description may perhaps do no other good than hitch the unknown unto something which is known and in this manner help to decipher the secret.

The more one studies nature the more clearly does he see that everything has a granular structure. There are the granules of matter, the atoms and molecules. Then there are the granules of electricity, the positive and the negative electrons. Then, again, there are the granules of organic life, the cells and the millions and millions of their constituent parts. Finally there are the nations with their millions of human granules. Each granule has an individual and more or less autonomous existence. A chaotic, a non-co-ordinated, activity results unless co-ordinators are introduced which transform the chaos into a cosmos. I do not think that I am too optimistic when I say that some day Carnot's Principle will help us to understand these complex activities of life in the same way that it has helped us to understand the phenomena of heat, radiation, and chemical action. At any rate, I do not see any other scientific principle which unites better the activities of the inorganic and organic world under one general and all-embracing concept.

VII

CREATIVE CO–ORDINATION

I

I HAVE a story to tell you and I hope that it will deliver to you a message from physical science which was delivered to me in the course of the last fifty years.

Fifty-two years ago I found my first employment in a factory in New York. That was my first opportunity to learn how to manage a boiler-room and its engine, and I gladly took it. It gave me the first lesson which taught me that the fire under the boiler supplies the driving-power to every machine in the factory in which I was employed. To an untutored Serbian immigrant who had never seen such things in his native village, that was an awe-inspiring knowledge, and it thrilled me. It stirred my emotions and my imagination, and I almost became a fire-worshipper.

A little later I had a brief experience in a foundry, where castings were made by pouring white-hot metal into suitable moulds in the chilling sand. I shall never forget the dazzling brilliancy of the white-hot metal made fluid by the breath of the roaring furnace flames, and the beautiful castings into which the white-hot metal was chilled and tempered. This was the second thrill which aroused my interest in the phenomena of heat.

When a youth is really thrilled by the beauty of a physical phenomenon he has many questions to ask. Many a youth in the land will ask you to-day: What is electricity? His thrilling experience with a radio-receiving set suggests the question. My thrilling experience in the boiler-room and in the foundry made me ask the questions: What is heat? How does it supply the driving-power? How does it shape and temper the metal castings? Questions of this kind are the beginning of a true interest in science, and such an interest permits no delay of the search for an answer. I searched for an answer in a book which was very popular in those days; it was Tyndall's famous book entitled: "Heat a Mode of Motion." It told me a wonderful story of the phenomena of heat. Tyndall's story was, I thought, a scientific poem in prose.

II

Now here is a bit of Tyndall's poetic story; it says: A hot and radiant body like the familiar flame under the boiler, and the white-hot metal in the foundry, are the seat of violent and erratic molecular motions. The higher the temperature the more intense is this erratic motion. Each one of the billions and billions of tiny molecules, like frantic individuals in a panicky crowd, is moving with aimless hurry, apparently following its own sweet will, and, therefore, colliding with its neighbors incessantly.

But you will say: "This is indeed an ugly chaos, and what thrill was there in the contemplation of such a chaos which made you think that Tyndall's description of it was poetry in prose?" Yes, it is a chaos, but it is a chaos in the microcosm, in the invisible world of atoms and molecules of the hot body. From this chaos there rose like a vision a new meaning of an old idea, the idea of temperature. Tyndall revealed it to me when he showed that temperature stands for the average energy of the chaotic molecular motion, which is the caloric energy of the body. The motion of heat from

[228]

points of higher to points of lower temperature, a well-known physical fact, appeared to me then in a new light. I described it as a motion of caloric energy from points of higher to points of lower energy levels similar to the motion of material bodies from points of higher to points of lower gravitational energy levels. My favorite question: How does the fire under the boiler supply the driving-power to every machine in the factory in which I was employed? was then easily answered as follows: Just as the mountain stream in its downward flow can drive a mill, so can heat, moving from the higher temperature level of the boiler to the lower temperature level of the condenser, drive the piston of the steam-engine and the machinery connected with it. But, guided by Tyndall, I did not press this analogy too far. One fundamental difference was obvious. There is no chaotic energy distribution among the particles of the water which drives the mill; each drop of the busy stream moves in orderly fashion alongside of its neighboring drops, and all of them, like an army of peaceful and well-drilled toilers, push in unison against the rotating wheel. This is a picture of a perfectly co-ordinated effort. But how about the chaotic push of the molecules of steam in the cylinder of a steam-engine? The piston receives the chaotic impacts of the vanishingly small but enormously numerous projectiles, the steam molecules, and averages them up, and thus co-ordinates their propelling force, the pressure of steam. The piston co-ordinates the action of a chaotic mob and transforms a part of the chaotic energy of steam into an orderly motion of the piston and of all the machinery connected with it. The piston is a co-ordinator. It is a *creative co-ordinator* because it creates a manageable motion of machinery out of an unmanageable molecular chaos. Just as the word "temperature" reminded me that heat is a molecular chaos, so the word "co-ordinator" reminded me that this chaos can be transformed into orderly motion, which the hand of man can manage and derive useful service. This is the simplest illustration of the service rendered by the co-ordination of the caloric chaos, by the harnessing of heat.

III

This was the revelation which Tyndall's book disclosed to me at the time when I was preparing for college. This preparation told me of a legend of ancient Greece, which says that in the beginning this world was a chaos, and that the Olympian gods had transformed it into a cosmos, a universe of simple law and beautiful order. I saw in the co-ordinating action of the piston a striking illustration of the creative process which the poetic soul of ancient Greece had reserved for the Olympian gods. "The prosy modern piston," said I, "imitates the Olympian deities; it transforms a chaos into a cosmos." The poets of ancient Greece would have credited the inventor of the steam-engine with the possession of a secret art which he had stolen from the Olympian gods, just as Prometheus had stolen the celestial fire from Helios. Yes, the modern inventor might be called a modern Prometheus who had stolen a secret from golden Helios, the sun-god. His steam-engine imitates the operation of the central star of our planetary system. Where the ancient worshippers of Helios saw a resplendent sun-god radiating his breath of life to the terrestrial waters, the modern inventor saw a celestial fire, and imitated its action upon the terrestrial waters by a fire under the boiler. Where the ancients saw the blessings of the sun-god manifesting themselves by the rising vapors lifted on high from rivers, lakes, and oceans, and forming clouds which, journeying to higher elevations of the terrestrial globe, carry the waters to the thirsty continents, there the modern inventor saw the motion of steam from the boiler to the condenser and on its journey driving the piston. The piston reacts against the chaotic impacts of the molecules of steam just as the weight of the cloud-forming vapors reacts against the chaotic pulses of solar radiation.

But neither the poets of ancient Greece nor the modern inventor detected in this cyclic motion of water a fundamental process of nature. They did not recognize in the motion of the gigantic water-masses a continuous transformation of the chaotic radiant energy of our central star into a huge storage of gravitational energy associated with the elevated water-masses. This energy is just as co-ordinated and available as the energy of the moving machinery which puzzled me fifty years ago. It descends to lower levels when the water-masses start their return journey to the oceans, and it is ready then to work for the miller on the mountainside, or for the husbandman, irrigating his thirsty fields in the blessed valley. This beautiful cyclic process is a transformation of a solar chaos into a terrestrial cosmos by the co-ordinating forces which reside in the primordial granules of water, in its atoms and molecules, and it was revealed by modern science. Tyndall revealed it to me, and this revelation enabled me to answer the questions: What is heat? and, How does the fire under the boiler supply the driving-power to every machine in the factory in which I was employed?

IV

Did it enable me also to answer the other question, namely: What is the mission of heat in the foundry where castings are made by pouring white-hot metal into a tempering mould in the chilling sand? Let the familiar snowflakes answer this question. They are the beautiful crystalline castings of the fluid-masses raised on high by the solar furnace and tempered by the chilling action of the surrounding space. The transformation of a tiny bit of shapeless water-vapor into the crystalline beauty of a snowflake is a transformation of a chaos into a cosmos. The chaos is the chaotic motion of the vapor molecules, the beautiful cosmos in the snowflake structure appears when the chilling process of the environment reduces this chaotic motion, and thus permits the atomic and molecular forces to co-ordinate the vapor molecules and assign to each its proper place in the stable structure of the snowflake crystals. This is a process of co-ordination in which the internal forces act as co-ordinators; it is their action which makes the snowflake crystals rise from the shapeless water-vapor just as beautiful Aphrodite rose from the shapeless foam of a turbulent sea. I never watch the graceful descent of the tiny snowflakes without recalling to memory those puzzling questions which many years ago I formulated in the boiler-room and in the foundry and, guided by Tyndall's poetic story, found this simple answer: Transformation of the caloric chaos into a cosmos of motion and of stable structures.

This creative process is exhibited beautifully in the evolution of matter in the galaxy of the blazing stars. There we still see an infant universe in its cradle. Many of the visible stars are white-hot bodies; some of them are in a state of a tenuous gas. This is the state of stellar infancy. The spectrum of these stellar infants tells us that at the lofty temperature levels of the hottest stars the lightest atoms only exist; so violent are the incessant molecular collisions in their everlasting chaos. But from this lofty temperature level each of them radiates its almost inexhaustible energy of caloric chaos at a lavish rate into the chilliness of the interstellar space. Like the vapor, coalescing into beautiful snowflakes or the white-hot metal moulded by the chilling sand into tempered castings, these tenuous stars are coalescing and some time, but God only knows when and where, they will form stable structures; call them celestial snowflakes, or celestial castings, whatever suits your fancy better.

Our terrestrial globe is a celestial casting, and he who like myself learned the language of the foundry in his early youth will ask the human question: What is the mission of this celestial casting, this old celestial wanderer through the mighty stream of chaotic solar radiation? Is it only to receive its final tempering from the solar furnace which gave it its birth, and to smooth out its jagged surface by the erosive action of the waters which solar radiation carries in ceaseless succession of cycles from the oceans to the higher continental elevations? The answer to this human question is obvious; it is this: The highest mission of this celestial casting, which we call affectionately "our mother earth," is to provide a congenial home for a new universe, "the universe of organic life."

V

He who in his early youth was thrilled by the phenomena of heat in the boiler-room and in the foundry and, guided by Tyndall, found in every nook and corner of the inorganic universe a continuous transformation of a microcosmic chaos into a visible cosmos will naturally look for a similar transformation in the universe of organic life. Such transformations are certainly there, and they give a definite meaning to the adjective "organic." They are, in my humble opinion, the most characteristic attributes of the physical activities in the organic universe.

Just as electricity is granular, consisting of electrons and protons; and inorganic matter is granular, consisting of atoms and molecules; so are also the caloric, the radiant, and the chemical energies granular since they manifest themselves through activities of the granules of electricity and matter. In this sense life, from a physical point of view, is also granular in structure, consisting of tiny granules of living matter; its physical activity is also granular, being made up of the activity of the granules of living matter. The organic universe, being a structure made up of countless tiny units, each of them endowed with individual power of action, will be a chaos just like the inorganic universe unless these units are guided by an inherent power of co-ordination.

The organic just like the inorganic universe has its microcosm, the fundamental units of which are not electrons and protons, atoms and molecules, but tiny units of life; call them, for want of a better name, the molecules of life, and by that I mean the microscopic and ultramicroscopic units of life in the living cell. Each of them feeds, grows, and multiplies, and that means a transformation of chemical and caloric energy delivered to it, and utilized for co-ordinated creative work, which is as definite as the constructive processes in an industrial plant. The similarity of this microcosmic performance to the procedure of supplying food, raw material, and co-ordinated power to the trained workers in a factory is certainly very suggestive. Chemical activities, when unguided by co-ordinating forces, are just as chaotic as caloric activity. Since these two activities supply the energy and the materials for co-ordinated constructive efforts to each molecule of life, that energy in its journey to this busy worker must, therefore, meet somewhere during this journey the reaction of a co-ordinator, just as the chaotic heat energy, in its journey from the boiler to the condenser, meets the reaction of the co-ordinating piston. Although we do not know the structure of this co-ordinator in the unit of life nor its co-ordinating steps, we can say, nevertheless, that co-ordinators and co-ordination are the characteristic attributes of the activity of each living molecule, each fundamental unit of life. This obviously is also the characteristic attribute of the activity of each cell as a whole; because it grows and multiplies in a perfectly orderly fashion at the expense of caloric and chemical energies. Each cell, therefore, is a microcosm consisting of a vast number of tiny units of life, all working alongside of each other like peaceful and disciplined toilers having a definite and common end in view. That end is the creation of new cells, performing definite functions. The structure of the new cells, the daughter cells, resembles that of the mother cells, but it is carefully adjusted with reference to the functions which the cells are destined to perform in the organic body. This is creative co-ordination according to our definition, because it is a transformation of a chaos, caloric and chemical, into orderly structures performing orderly functions.

Finally, each autonomous organic structure, the organic body, is a macrocosm, an aggregation of a vast number of cellular microcosms; it displays the same co-ordinated activity as each of its fundamental units. Co-ordinators and co-ordination, in the sense in which these concepts have been defined here, are, therefore, the most characteristic strokes of the brush which paints our mental pictures of the structure of the organic as well as of the inorganic universe. The two pictures exhibit a striking resemblance to each other. But in the inorganic universe we know the structure of the co-ordinators and many details of their co-ordinating functions; in the organic, however, we do not know them. We know the results of their operations, but we do not know the various co-ordinating steps which lead to this result, not even in so simple a process as fermentation. We cannot say to-day that these steps are of a purely mechanical nature, as in the case of the inorganic universe, nor can science deny it. Suppose, however, that some day we do succeed in demonstrating that the co-ordinators in the molecules of life and in their cellular microcosms are physical structures similar to and operating in a way similar to those in the inorganic universe, that will not mean a victory for the mechanistic view of life. There will still remain the mystery of the living soul and of its internal world, particularly that of the living soul of man. Can the language of science describe the creative process which brings this internal world into existence without employing the vocabulary of speculative philosophy? An affirmative answer to this question is suggested by the thoughts concerning creative co-ordination described in this narrative.

VI

Our mother earth is a tiny dust speck in the material universe, but as the home of the creative soul of man it becomes the crown of creation. The life of man is, as far as we know, the highest product of creation, and it is the most precious gift of heaven. Its broadest aspect is co-ordination, which eliminates the chaos from the activities of its countless molecules of life, and constructs the cosmos, the presence of which we feel in the internal world of our creative soul, our consciousness; in the language of science it might be described as "the climax of creative co-ordination." Its cosmos is probably the ideal cosmos which the poets of ancient Greece had in mind when they represented it as the creation of the Olympian gods.

No scientist can contemplate the mighty theme, the life of man, without pausing reverently and recalling Tennyson's well-known lines, dedicated to a tiny flower plucked from the crannied wall:

"I hold thee here, root and all, in my hand,
    Little flower—but if I could understand
What you are, root and all, and all in all,
    I should know what God and man is."

[241]

No words of mortal man can describe more beautifully the mystery of organic life. Can the knowledge for which Tennyson was yearning be advanced even a tiny bit if the life of man is viewed in the light of the cosmic processes of creative co-ordination? Such an attempt is not without some promise.

Paderewski's vibrating fingers speeding along the keyboard like electric waves through quiescent space arouse my emotions, and I wonder at the harmonious response of the billions and billions of organic cells to the co-ordinating physical processes which animate Paderewski's ethereal touch. But my wonder is amplified a thousandfold when I listen to the tuneful message which this performance of perfect physical co-ordination conveys to me from the internal world of Paderewski's consciousness, where it was recorded by the creative soul of some heaven-born genius. I cannot resist, then, crossing the boundary-line which separates the external material world from the internal world of my consciousness. Here I find a power which is at work creating this internal world; this power is a manifestation of a new entity in the existence of which mankind always believed and called it the soul of man. This belief is the essence extracted from all human experience. No physical reality rests upon a broader and deeper foundation of experience than this belief. The soul is the creative co-ordinator residing in the body of man and guiding its functions so as to make the life of man a cosmos, a creation of simple law and beautiful order. Our belief in the existence of the creative soul is the origin of our belief in the existence of a Creator. Our present knowledge derived from man's experience ever since he began to live a human life rejects the hypothesis that the creative power of man's consciousness is the highest form of creative co-ordination; it demands a still higher form of creative co-ordination. The creative power residing in us is, therefore, the origin of the belief that our creative soul is a part of Him who endowed the electrons and protons, the atoms and molecules, and the tiniest units of living matter with those primordial attributes which manifest themselves in the cosmic processes called in this narrative creative co-ordination.

VII

Never did man exhibit more clearly the divine origin of his soul than when he began to recognize that his life is a part, only, of a much more complex and significant life, the life of humanity, the life of an enormous number of autonomous individuals each facing daily the struggle for existence. To guide this complex life from a threatening chaos of a non-co-ordinated humanity to a social cosmos became then the highest problem of man's creative soul. The gradual solution of this problem is the evolution of social co-ordinators, which promised to lead humanity to a social cosmos. Church and State are the most important among the social co-ordinators; they are, like the physical structure of the human body, physical structures only, employed in co-ordinating operations. But just as the human body becomes a living soul when it is animated by the divine breath of its Creator, so the same divine breath must give to Church and State a living soul which will guide their operations and put into them the power of that creative co-ordination which will lead the life of humanity to a cosmos. That soul is the co-ordinated effort of our individual souls, guided by the highest ideals of spiritual achievement. Without such efforts the life of humanity will never rise to the full glory of a social cosmos, and the individual life of man, the most precious gift of heaven, will lose many blessings to which it is entitled by its close relationship to the divinity of the Creator, the fountainhead of all spiritual realities.

Just as the cosmic processes of creative co-ordination guide the evolution of the external material world, so creative co-ordination also guides the evolution of the internal world of the human soul, the destiny of human life. This is my message from science.

I cannot close this story without adding a message which I delivered last October to the students of Vassar College and of Kenyon College. It is as follows:

A MESSAGE OF SOUND AND LIGHT

In my boyhood days I used to spend a part of my school vacation attending to my father's herd of several oxen. My schoolmates rendered a similar service to the herds of their fathers, and some twelve of us joined our small herds into a large one. The oldest of the boys was the master herdsman and the rest of us were his assistants. Watching a herd at night is a strenuous art. We had to keep awake and watch every step of the grazing oxen, lest they should go astray and be stolen by the cattle thieves who lay in wait in the endless cornfields and watched for their opportunity. The appetite of the grazing ox is regulated by the hours of the night, and we anxiously watched the progress of the advancing darkness and the gradual approach of the joyful dawn. The blazing stars of the black firmament of the summer night told us by their position the hour of the night. I imagined that the light of those stars was a message from God which helped us to guard our grazing herd. The faint sound of the clock of the distant and slumbering village was another welcome message which, like the message of the stars, aided us in our watchfulness, and thus I gradually began to imagine that the sound of the church bell was also a message from God. My mother, who was a pious woman, encouraged me in this belief. Whenever the vesper-bell announced that the village priest was about to commence the vesper service my mother would say: "Michael, do you not hear the divine message which calls you to church to assist the priest in his service at the altar of God?" I listened and obeyed the message.

It is not surprising that in my boyhood days I often put two questions to myself. One question was: What is sound? and the other, What is light? A search for an answer to these two questions directed my scientific career.

WHAT IS SOUND?

Permit me now to tell you briefly the answer to the first question, the question, namely: What is sound? This will prepare us for my answer to the second question.

When the clapper strikes the church bell the bell vibrates and transmits its vibration to the air; the sound-waves in the air, spreading out in every direction, reach the listening ear, and convey to the inquiring mind of man the following simple story: The collision between the clapper and the bell puts

[247]

energy into the bell, and, feeding upon this energy, the bell becomes a living thing. Its life manifests itself through its vibrations, which are in harmony with its structure. Neither the clapper nor the power which moves it can change the character of these vibrations. They are the result of the elasticity and the density of the material of which the bell is made, and of its form which the designing intelligence of the bell-maker gave it.

But does that story give us a complete description of this familiar illustration of sound generation, transmission, and perception? No, it does not; it says nothing about the message which the bell is conveying to our souls. To get this part of the story we must follow the vibrations in their passage through that marvellous receiving instrument, the ear, which, with its sixty thousand parts, is busy speeding the message along millions of tiny nerves to the central station, the brain. There the soul of man interprets the language of the bell. This second part of the story of the bell tells me that the vibrating bell is a small link only in the endless chain of phenomena which connect the external physical world to the internal world of our soul, where the message of the bell is deciphered. The more I study this second part of the story of the bell the more I recognize to-day that my boyhood fancy was right when on the pasture-lands of my native village it led me to imagine that the faint sound of the distant village clock was a message from God.

I never listen to the melodies of Kreisler's violin without recalling to mind this message of nearly sixty years ago. To me Kreisler's violin is a bell. The smooth and silent movement of his bow communicates to the strings a rapid succession of tiny pulses identical in action to the strokes of the clapper upon the church bell. They are tiny but numerous clappers which impart to the strings the energy of their life. This life manifests itself in their melodious vibrations, carrying a wonderful tale to our listening soul. The tale is identical with that which I recited to you in my description of the language of the church bell. But one essential difference must be mentioned. The violin-maker, just like the maker of the church bell, imparts to the bell, called the violin, its fundamental character. The virtues of a Stradivarius are among the

[249]

glories of human ingenuity. But the temperament and skill of a Kreisler superpose upon this fundamental character of the violin an almost infinite variety of modulations. Kreisler makes the vibrating strings speak a language which is indeed a message from heaven. When Kreisler plays a Beethoven sonata he is the apostle of the great composer and delivers his master's message. The message is the embodiment of an inspiration the cradle of which is the soul of the heaven-born genius. Such a message from Kreisler's violin is a message from divinity and it recalls to my memory the vesper-bell of my native village and my mother's words: "Michael, do you not hear God's message which calls you to his altar to praise his everlasting glory?"

This is the answer which science gave me to the question: What is sound?

WHAT IS LIGHT?

Permit me now to tell you briefly my answer to the second question, the question, namely: What is light? This is indeed a momentous question. The sun-worship among the ancients testifies that even without a trace of the scientific knowledge which we possess to-day, the ancients knew intuitively the function of sunlight in all organic life. They knew that without this source of life-giving radiation our terrestrial globe would be a cold and dreary desert.

The greatest glory of science of the nineteenth century is the discovery that light is an electromagnetic phenomenon. To Faraday and to Maxwell and to their native land, the British Isles, belongs that glory. What is the meaning of this wonderful discovery? It is very simple; indeed, it is simplicity itself. A ray of light from our sun or from any hot and luminous body is a swarm of an enormous, practically infinite, number of tiny electrical dots and dashes speeding along through space just like the electrical dots and dashes which the wireless telegraph stations send through space, or which the ordinary telegraphers send along wires. Each atom and molecule in the blazing sun is a busy radio station sending messages in all directions. These countless dots and dashes tell us that countless tiny electrical clappers are set in motion by the atoms and molecules of the

radiating source. Now, what do I mean by that?
Consider what you are doing when you are ring-
ing a telephone bell. You transmit a rapid succession of electrical pulses along the telephone
wire, that is to say, a rapid succession of impulsive
electronic motions. The moving electrons are the
electrical clappers; each moving electronic swarm
gives a jerk at the clapper of the telephone bell, and
makes it strike; the bell responds with a ring. The
action of the electrical clappers is thus transformed
into the action of a material clapper. The dots
and dashes coming from busy atoms and molecules
of the sun are a rapid succession of electrical pulses;
they, like the electrical pulses which ring the telephone bell, strike the material bodies on earth and
communicate to their atoms and molecules the energy of their life. Like the bell on the church spire
of my native village, or like the melodious strings
of Kreisler's violin, these terrestrial aggregations of
atoms and molecules respond and radiate vibrations which are in harmony with their structure.
They are the receiving instruments for the messages transmitted by the luminous bodies.

In telegraphy we have a code, that is a certain

number of combinations of dots and dashes, each combination standing for a definite word or letter, and the receiving instrument responds equally well to each combination. In a ray of sunlight there are an infinite number of combinations of dots and dashes, and it cannot be expected that each terrestrial body will respond equally well to every one of them. We can say that the terrestrial bodies are bells, responding best to electrical pulses of some definite form. For instance, this rose responds to electronic pulses which make it sing out: "I am red," and that rose sings out "I am yellow" when struck by another type of radiant clapper. The lily responds equally well to all of them and sings out: "I am white." Christ, as quoted by St. Matthew, felt the thrill of a true scientist when, beholding the lily, he exclaimed:

Consider the lilies how they grow; they toil not, neither do they spin; and yet I say unto you that Solomon in all his glory was not arrayed like one of these.

Each tiny flower of the field is a little bell responsive to some solar clappers, and so is the brilliant cloud figure which bids good-by to the setting sun or announces the approach of the early dawn. The whole terrestrial globe is a cosmic bell which, responding to the strokes of the solar clappers, glorifies the beauties of our mother earth. But that is one part only of the message which the sun and the luminous stars are sending to us. Each signalling atom in the sun and in the luminous stars sends us the history of its life and of the life of the star to which it belongs. Listen to a message which the spectroscope reports from a young star somewhere near the very boundary of our stellar system. The message says: "I am a million light years away from you. I am an astral baby now, and will be a baby still when a million years hence you receive this message. Many billions of years will pass before the ardor of my youth has cooled down to the moderation of your central star, the sun. Heaven only knows when I shall be as old as your old mother earth. But when I reach that age I shall be a beautiful cosmic bell just like your earth and responding to the clappers of the luminous stars, I shall add my voice to the celestial choir which is declaring the glory of God."

This is my answer to the question, What is light?

The answer was prepared in the world of the human soul where a divine creative power resides, and it recalls to memory the faint strokes of the vesper-bell of my native village of sixty years ago and my mother's voice saying: "Michael, do you not hear the divine message which calls you to the altar of the almighty God?"

EPILOGUE

THESE narratives are guided by an obvious aim. It is to find a short and easy journey from the physical realities of the inorganic to those of the organic world, and then finally to the realities in the world of our consciousness. The ultimate object of the journey is also obvious; it is to illustrate the spiritual realities in the world of human consciousness by the physical realities of the external physical world. The journey can, therefore, be called a journey "from physical to spiritual realities."

When the primordial activities in the physical universe, as described in these narratives, revealed themselves as the activities of a practically infinite number of tiny granules, electrons and protons, atoms and molecules, organic cells and their constituent molecules of life, then the picture of an all-embracing cosmic chaos of activities presented itself; the activities of enormous swarms of autonomous granules is necessarily chaotic. Alongside of this puzzling picture, the narratives presented also the familiar pictures of orderly creations rising everywhere from the cosmic chaos, just like so many blissful islands of beautiful order, rising out of the chaotic turbulence of a storm-tossed ocean. These orderly creations reminded us that there is in every nook and corner of the physical universe a transformation of the primordial chaos into an orderly and intelligible cosmos. This transformation is the most characteristic feature of the world of organic life. Its operation is called in these narratives a Creative Co-ordination; it is an interpreter and guide to the narratives on their journey from the inorganic to the organic world, and finally to the world of human consciousness.

Creative Co-ordination, mentioned so frequently in these narratives, is not a metaphysical abstraction; it is a familiar physical process which meets us everywhere. The steam-engine and the snowflake; the cycles of the moving water masses which carry their blessings to the thirsty terrestrial continents; the growth of plants and of animals—they all tell the same simple story of Creative Co-ordination. It is a physical operation defined in terms of definite physical laws, and it exhibits a progressive advance from lower to higher forms of orderly structures and functions in the organic as well as in the inorganic world; a continuous rise from lower to higher levels of creation.

When the narratives pass from the external physical world to the internal world of consciousness then again Creative Co-ordination is a welcome interpreter and guide. It is only in the light which this interpreter and guide throws upon the phenomena of consciousness that the narratives discuss this abstract subject which is obviously somewhat foreign to exact physical sciences. To illustrate: The beauty of the sunset, a living picture of joy in the world of our consciousness, is the ultimate product of a creative co-ordination. The radiation of the setting sun, reflected, refracted, and scattered by matter floating in the atmosphere, is the external source of this beauty. It is an energy chaos, a practically infinite number and variety of electrical pulses sent out at random by the busy solar electrons. These chaotic signals are recorded by our sensations and appear in our consciousness as the beauty of the sunset, a cosmos of consciousness, a creation called into existence by the chaotic energy supply of the external world. This is creative co-ordination, which connects the external physical world to the world of our consciousness.

The perfume of the rose, the comforting glow of the log in our fireplace, the ambrosial sweetness of the honey—are all orderly realities of pleasure and joy in the world of our consciousness, but they all can be traced to the chaotic stimuli of the external world. These few examples suffice to show that chaotic signals convey messages to the living body from its environment, but that each deciphered message appears as an intelligible cosmos in the world of consciousness. There is somewhere in the path of these messages a Creative Co-ordination which transforms their chaos into an intelligible cosmos of our consciousness.

A part of the co-ordinating transformation is obviously in the physical structure of our body which, like the piston of a steam-engine, averages up the chaotic pulses conveyed through a most complex network of nerves from the external world to the central station, the brain. But the resulting cosmos in the world of consciousness is not that of orderly physical structures performing orderly physical functions like those in the external inorganic and organic world; it is the cosmos of a state of consciousness. We cannot describe it in terms of any known physical realities; neither can we express it in terms of actions and reactions of any known physical entity. Hence we infer that the cosmos of consciousness is a manifestation of a new entity which we call the soul, just as from the manifestations of electrical and magnetic forces Faraday inferred the existence of new entities which these narratives call the electrical and the magnetic flux. The cosmos of consciousness is a psychic reality; it is subjective, of course, but it is as real to us as, for instance, the objective physical reality of electrical radiation. Just as electrical radiation reveals the existence of an ultra-material entity, the electrical flux, so the psychic realities of our consciousness reveal the existence of an ultra-material entity, the soul. The ultimate natures of these two entities are hidden behind a cosmic veil which so far has remained impenetrable; their manifestations, however, are perfectly clear; they are like a living embroidery of supremely subtle texture adorning the visible face of the cosmic veil. But just as Maxwell made many efforts to penetrate deeper into the meaning of Faraday's fluxes, so the many efforts to penetrate deeper into the meaning of the ultra-material entity called soul are perfectly natural. Its meaning interests human inquiry to-day just as much as it ever did since man began to observe and to reason.

At the very outset of these endeavors, however, the scientist meets a serious difficulty. He immediately detects a fundamental difference between the two ultra-material substances; one of them, the electrical flux, became a dynamically definite and hence perfectly intelligible physical entity when the laws of its actions and reactions were formulated in accordance with Newtonian dynamics and verified by electrical radiation experiments. The scientist looks for a similar intelligibility of the other ultra-material substance and he asks: Can a similar statement be made concerning the soul? Is the soul a dynamically definite entity? If it is not, what hope is there for the methods of scientific inquiry to make it so? In answer to these legitimate questions, we certainly can say that the soul acts and reacts, but we cannot say that its actions and reactions, like those of the electrical flux, can be expressed in terms of the Newtonian concepts of actions and reactions. The following consideration, however, is certainly reasonable: If the soul does not act and react, how does the beauty of the sunset appear in the world of our consciousness, or how do the objective physical realities, revealed by science during the last four hundred years, become subjective realities in the world of our consciousness? It would indeed be a very great achievement, if we could reduce these psychic actions and reactions, the operators of the creative power of the soul, to the simple laws of Newtonian dynamics, but why despair if we cannot? The actions and reactions of an individual radiating atom have not yet been reduced to the simplicity of Newton's dynamics, but that does not shake anybody's faith in the radiating power of the atom. Our faith in the creative power of the soul should be at least as strong, for surely the world of consciousness, the product of that creative power, is at least as real as atomic radia-

[263]

tion. The existence of this creative power is the most fundamental human experience in the course of centuries of centuries, so that to-day it is just as axiomatic as Newton's laws of motion, and it is a sufficient proof of the existence of the soul, although the actions and reactions of the soul are for the present and probably will remain forever entirely outside of Newtonian dynamics. Newton would be the last to claim that his science is the final word on actions and reactions in the world of phenomena. But does his science encourage the scientific man to engage in inquiries concerning actions and reactions which he apparently cannot subject to scientific methods of observation, experiment, and calculation? Let the following considerations answer this question.

The creative power of the soul is the only guide in our attempts to decipher the meaning of this ultra-material substance. It furnishes the most reliable standard of comparing the soul of one man with the soul of another man and with that of lower animals. This comparison, resembling, to some extent, the scientific methods of quantitative measurement, has been going on ever since civilization began. The procedure of this inquiry is in many ways equivalent to the scientific method of inquiry by observation, experiment, and calculation; what it lacks in precision it makes up by its vast number of trials and errors extending over many centuries of qualitative measurements by careful comparison. It resulted in the universal verdict, that not only is the soul of man far superior to the animal soul, but that this difference is immeasurably greater than the difference in their bodily structures. The comparison revealed also an element in this difference which towers high above all the other differentiating elements; it is the *spiritual* element. The creative power of the human soul has created a new world in human consciousness; it is the spiritual world. Perhaps something resembling this spiritual world exists also in the consciousness of lower animals, but if it does there is no unmistakable sign of it in their conduct. There is, however, one most convincing evidence which speaks against the probability of this existence. *Man worships, animals do not;* spirituality and worship are inseparably associated according to all human experience.

Hence, when man began to worship, the embryo of the spiritual world began to form in his consciousness. This raised man by leaps and bounds above the level of lower animals. But man's worship is unthinkable without a recognition on his part that a creative power exists which is far superior to the creative power of his own soul. This recognition, the offspring of man's experience and reasoning, is the origin of our belief in God, the Creator. The influence of this belief upon the evolution of man's spiritual consciousness is beautifully described by St. Paul in the following words:

But we all, with open face beholding . . . the glory of the Lord, are changed into the same image from glory to glory.

Observation, experiment, and calculation led science to the revelation of new physical realities. This method of inquiry constructed the firm foundation of these realities, a foundation laid deeply in the solid ground of human experience. In a similar way, human experience, derived from contemplation and analysis of the creative power of the human soul, led human reason to the belief in God, the fountainhead of all spiritual realities.

The values of these realities fortified this belief. Their values in every action of human life are felt daily even more deeply than the values of physical realities. All human experience testifies that they are not mere shadows which mislead the untrained imagination. Newton, Faraday, Maxwell, Ampère, and many other great scientists believed strongly in spiritual realities. Have they been led astray on account of untrained imagination? The highest value of the spiritual realities is revealed in the longing of the human soul to rescue the life of humanity from a threatening chaos and transform it into a cosmos, a humanity of simple law and beautiful order, the nearest approach to what we Christians call the Kingdom of God. This longing for the cosmos of simple law and beautiful order in the life of humanity was undoubtedly planted in the human soul by its contemplation of the beautiful cosmos revealed by the realities of the physical world. The mighty oak, for instance, with its millions of leaves inhaling the life-giving energy of the golden sunshine, and with its millions of tiny roots exploring the nourishing wealth of the soil, all co-operating for one common end, is a beautiful physical illustration of the cosmos in the life of humanity. Such are the points of contact between physical and spiritual realities which lead us to the recognition of striking resemblances between these realities.

The individual man is a granule in the world of humanity. His relationship to the other granules of humanity and to the physical universe gives his life a definite meaning. This relationship is completely determined by his conduct. If the social cosmos, the Kingdom of God, is to appear on earth, then the conduct of the human granules must be guided toward that goal, just as the chaotic vapor molecules are guided by intrinsic forces when they coalesce into the cosmos of beautiful snowflake crystals. Creative Co-ordination, as defined by these narratives, is, therefore, the only process which will lift the life of humanity from chaos to cosmos, from lower to higher levels of creation, just as it transforms the chaos into a cosmos in every part of the granular inorganic and organic world, and in the activities of the chaotic energy granules which feed the physical roots of our consciousness. Creative Co-ordination is, therefore, the bridge which connects the world of physical to that of spiritual realities; it is the guide from lower to higher levels of creation in the physical as well as in the spiritual world. This is the first of the resemblances between these realities. Let us approach the second.

Creative Co-ordination is unthinkable unless there are intrinsic forces acting upon the chaotic granules which are to be co-ordinated; these forces are the co-ordinators, as these narratives call them. History records innumerable evidences which testify that among the co-ordinating forces in the life of man and of humanity the spiritual forces are the most powerful co-ordinators. The similarity in the co-ordinating operations of physical forces to those of the spiritual forces is the second resemblance between physical and spiritual realities.

The testimony of Christ is, according to our Christian belief, by far the most convincing of all the testimonies relating to the co-ordinating action of the spiritual forces. The arguments supporting this belief appeal to our reason with the same force as the arguments supporting a well-established physical theory. Our Christian knowledge of the spiritual forces revealed by Christ is deeply rooted in the solid ground of human experience of nearly two thousand years; it is a house built upon the hard rock of experience, and not upon the shifting sands of arbitrary hypotheses. This knowledge, like scientific knowledge, is the extract of innumerable observations and experiments recorded in the history of human lives; it is, therefore, just as carefully tested and as trustworthy as our knowledge of physical forces. Dealing as it does with the laws of actions and reactions of spiritual forces, it may be called spiritual dynamics. Christ created it long before Newton had announced his dynamics of matter in motion, Maxwell his electrodynamics, and Carnot his thermodynamics. These dynamical sciences deal with the physical world; Christ's dynamics deals with the spiritual world. The dynamical sciences of the physical world are naturally incomparably simpler than the dynamics of the spiritual world, but their mutual resemblance both in form and in evolutionary growth is obvious. This resemblance finds the simplest and most striking illustration in the efforts of the spiritual forces to transform the life of humanity into a cosmos, a living structure of simple law and beautiful order. It is here that the mode of operation of the co-ordinating spiritual forces reminds us most vividly of the mode of operation of the co-ordinating physical forces, and this exhibits the most obvious resemblance between physical and spiritual realities.

Our Christian faith sees in the life and the teaching of Christ the highest spiritual reality which our belief in God, the fountainhead of all spiritual realities, planted in the soul of man. This reality, we believe, endowed our souls with the spiritual forces which guide us in the spiritual co-ordination of each individual life and of the life of humanity. Love, according to Christ, is the most powerful of all these co-ordinating forces. Its co-ordinating action in the spiritual world is very similar to the co-ordinating action of the gravitational force in the physical world. Christ discovered it and revealed it to us in His two commandments:

Thou shalt love the Lord thy God with all thy heart, and with all thy soul, and with all thy mind.
Thou shalt love thy neighbor as thyself.

These commandments are the fundamental law in Christ's spiritual dynamics. It is obvious that under the guidance of this law we can liberate ourselves from the dominating love of purely material things and thus rescue our own individual lives and the life of humanity from the threatening chaos, and transform it into a cosmos, a life of simple law and beautiful order.

Creative Co-ordination leads, therefore, to a higher level of creation by the action of spiritual forces, just as it does in the physical world by the action of physical forces. It is the concept of this universal co-ordinating process which unites the two worlds to each other, so that our understanding of one will aid our understanding of the other. The cultivation of this view is encouraged by the following words of St. Paul addressed to the Romans:

For the invisible things of Him from the creation of the world are clearly seen, being understood by the things that are made, even His eternal power and Godhead.

Yes, God's spiritual realities are invisible, but they are illustrated and made intelligible by the physical realities revealed in the physical things which are made. According to this interpretation of the Apostle's words the physical and the spiritual realities supplement each other. They are the two terminals of the same realities; one terminal residing in the human soul, and the other in the things of the external world. Here is one of the fundamental reasons why Science and Religion supplement each other. They are the two pillars of the portal through which the human soul enters the world where the divinity resides. This is the mental attitude which dictated these narratives. If the signs of the times do not deceive then there is a universal drift toward this mental attitude. This drift I call The New Reformation.